Reg Andlaw was born in Gibralta⌐
Gibraltarian. During the Second V
with his family first to Casablanca, t ⸻, ⸻ ⸻ moving
to Tangier. In 1944 he was sent to school in England. He was edu-
cated at Oundle School and in 1957 graduated as a dentist from
Guy's Hospital. Following three years of postgraduate work at
the Eastman Dental Center in Rochester, New York, he settled in
Bristol and was a consultant senior lecturer in paediatric dentistry at the University of Bristol Dental School until he took
early retirement in December 1988. He continued as editor of the
International Journal of Paediatric Dentistry until 1997. He is married and has two daughters.

A
TRANS-IBERIAN
CHALLENGE
CYCLING THROUGH SPAIN

Reg Andlaw

COUNTRY BOOKS

Published by:
Country Books, Courtyard Cottage, Little Longstone, Bakewell, Derbyshire DE45 1NN

ISBN 1 898941 29 7

Cover pictures
Front: On the road to Plasencia
Rear: The Rock of Gibraltar

Acknowledgements
Thanks to Steve Sparrow for the back-cover photograph,
and to Harvey's Cycle Exchange, Bristol, from whom I obtained
a trusty bike and much helpful advice.

Design, typesetting & production: Country Books, Little Longstone, Derbyshire DE45 1NN

Printed & Bound by: MFP Design & Print, Stretford, Manchester M32 0JT

Cover origination by: GA Graphics, Stamford, Lincolnshire PE9 2RE

I dedicate this book to Roger,
my great friend, who died suddenly
18 months after leading the way
through Spain.

The route, overnight stops indicated

CONTENTS

INTRODUCTION
THE CHALLENGE

"Let's cycle across Europe to Gibraltar". The statement came out of the blue one autumn evening over a pint in a Somerset pub. I had learned over many years, since our student days together at Guy's Hospital, that Roger James was apt to come up with wild ideas, which were usually ignored or quickly dismissed, and this is what I did: after all, neither of us had sat on a bicycle since we were teenagers and we were now in our 60s. But it became clear over the following weeks that he was serious and therefore that I was faced with a challenge. During our student days, when we shared a dingy room at the top of a Victorian terrace in Bayswater, I had to face fierce challenges from him in a wide variety of activities, ranging from the common pub games — darts, pool, table football — to extraordinary games of cricket and golf contested in our room. For cricket we thrashed a squash ball around the room with a handled clothes brush, defending a litter-bin wicket (to this day I feel pangs of guilt when I think of how we must have disturbed the dear old lady who lived on the floor below); for golf the ball was putted more quietly round a course determined by conveniently-spaced holes in the worn-out carpet. In more recent years the challenges have involved more recognized sports, ranging from tennis to windsurfing, but long-distance cycling was a new one. How could I refuse to rise to it? I did, however, gain one concession: to make it a trans-Iberian trip, starting in Santander, rather than a trans-European one.

Our wives considered that this was one of Roger's crazy ideas, that we were too old to embark on such a trip, and that we should stay at home and do the gardening. After protracted negotiations we were reluctantly given the go-ahead, on condition that we agreed to stay together so as to be on hand should one or the other collapse by the roadside.

Many would not rate cycling from Santander to Gibraltar as a

1

serious challenge — similar, and much longer, cycle journeys are commonplace — but for us, sexagenarians who had not cycled since our youth, it was a challenge. Both of us had recently taken slightly-early retirement and were reasonably fit and determined to remain active, but I was not at all sure that I could cycle across Spain. I reassured myself with the thoughts that hills can always be negotiated on foot and that, if the going got too tough, hopping on to a train or bus would ease the pain.

The reason for choosing Gibraltar as our destination is simple: I am a Gibraltarian, although resident for many years in England. My life in Gibraltar was interrupted first by the Second World War (when all women and children, and men not performing an essential job, were evacuated) and later by school and university in England, but my family returned to the Rock after the war. We could, therefore, be sure of receiving tender loving care should we arrive a little the worse for wear.

The first essential was to buy bicycles. We were both, independently, advised to choose a 'hybrid', which combines features of the mountain and road bike. The next essential was to get on and not fall off. It is always said that one never forgets how to ride a bike, and I found this to be true up to a point, but initially I felt extremely clumsy and uncertain, especially in using the 21 gears and in sliding my feet under or out of the pedal straps. The last bicycle I owned, many years ago, had three gears at most, and no pedal straps. Using the range of gears correctly on my new machine took some practice, and I soon learned that forgetting to free at least one foot from the strap before coming to a halt inevitably resulted in a sideways crash to the ground. Both of us admitted to suffering this indignity more than once — luckily not falling either in the path of a bus or (almost as serious) within sight of those who had questioned the wisdom of our plans.

Our practice and training were very limited. Roger climbed on to the Mendip Hills a few times from his home in Wells, and I rode up to the Durdham and Clifton Downs from mine in Bristol, but these were exercises more about gaining confidence in handling the bicycles than about physical conditioning. We had bought the bikes in January and planned to be off in mid-April:

more time would have been needed for serious training. Our trip was to be a test of our existing level of fitness — and, perhaps, of other attributes.

Using the 1/400,000 (1cm:4km) series of Michelin maps (numbers 442, 444 and 446) we made a general plan to follow a course down the west of Spain, because the altitude of the *sierras* that stretch east-west across the country tends to decrease towards the west; we did not want to make the trip any harder than it had to be. For guidance regarding accommodation we relied on *Spain: The Rough Guide* (which also provides useful and interesting information on all aspects of travel in Spain). The Spanish Tourist Office in London sent some leaflets, most of which were unrelated to my specific enquiries. But the most interesting and helpful source of information was a book by Robin Neillands entitled *Walking Through Spain*. Neillands walked from near Santander to Gibraltar in 6 weeks, following a route a little to the east of ours, much of it off-road. Although a walker's requirements are somewhat different from a cyclist's, the book contained useful guidance on preparing for the trip, down to the choice of clothes and equipment. (His kit list at the back of the book does not include the stick he stated elsewhere to be essential to fend off dogs; this had me worried, but I decided to take a chance and do without one.) We travelled very light: just two panniers each, slung on each side of the back wheel. Mine weighed only 11 pounds each, containing only what I thought were bare essentials — which later I found was more than I really needed.

The book is an account of what was a most rewarding experience: not only was there the satisfaction of rising to the challenge and achieving our goal but also the fun of exploring the country and observing its people and their way of life.

CHAPTER 1
THE WELCOMING PICOS
PLYMOUTH TO SANTANDER
TO BARCENA DE PIÉ DE CONCHA

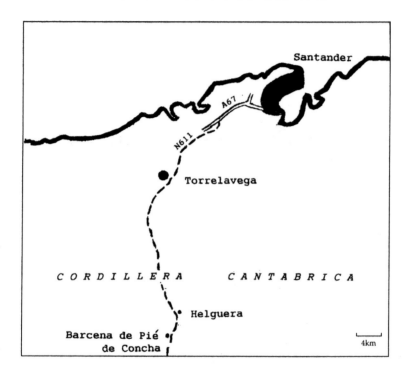

I travelled by train from Bristol to Plymouth on a beautiful morning in mid-April. As the train rolled past peaceful Somerset and Devon countryside and then skirted the tranquil Exe and Teign estuaries I asked myself what I was doing leaving all this behind to coop myself up in a ferry and then slog it out on Spanish roads. But there was no going back. At Plymouth station a brightly-coloured object caught my eye, which turned out to be none other than Roger in his cycling togs. It was only a short ride to the ferry terminal but it was a relief to get there, having managed to avoid getting flattened while negotiating heavy traffic on roundabouts, a hazard I had rather stupidly neglected to familiarize myself with during my very basic preparations at home. Ushered into a special queue for cyclists we immediately experienced the camaraderie of the cycling fraternity, comparing and discussing technical details of our bikes and trying to appear as if we knew what we were talking about.

The Brittany Ferries *Val de Loire*, launched in 1987, is a big and impressive ship: over 21,000 tons, 161 metres (530ft) long, carrying up to 2141 passengers and 600 cars, and cruising at 20 knots. Granted a reasonably smooth sea (which is by no means certain in the Bay of Biscay) a comfortable journey is assured. We left Plymouth at 12 noon and were due to arrive in Santander at noon (1 o'clock Spanish time) the next day. About $1^1/_2$ hours before landfall the coast first came into view, a faint dark band topped, to the west, with what at first looked like white clouds but which later could be identified as snow on the peaks of the Picos de Europa. The magnificent mountain panorama of the Cordillera Cantabrica, crowned by the famous Picos, provides a spectacular backdrop to this coast of Spain. Over the centuries, the sight of those mountains must have lifted the spirits of countless Spaniards returning home after a long absence, but perhaps none more so than the leader of the Spanish Armada, the Duke of Medina Sidonia, whose galleon the *San Martín* limped into Santander on the third day of September 1588, having been blown and battered by storms up the North Sea, around the Scottish islands and down the west coast of Ireland following the Armada's unsuccessful mission in the English Channel. We, on the other hand, had a smooth and relaxing crossing, but relax-

Riding on to the ferry

ation now turned to some anxiety at the prospect of crossing the mountains that lay ahead. Entering the beautiful bay of Santander, the royal palace, a castellated mansion built at the end of the last century by public subscription for Alfonso XIII, stands out on the Peninsula de la Magdalena, and beyond it stretch the wonderful golden beaches of El Sardinero. Santander is the capital of Cantabria and a popular holiday centre for Spaniards, becoming fashionable initially because of the king's occasional residence there.

During the crossing Roger unveiled our team shirt, bright yellow with the words *'El Viejo Equipo'* ('The Old Team') embroidered in blue across the left breast, *viejo* here alluding to the pedigree of the team, not to the age of its members (although some, not unreasonably, might have interpreted it in the latter sense).

"Car drivers and their passengers may now go down to their vehicles". The eagerly-awaited announcement generated sudden mass movement towards the stairways, and also some confusion among some, including myself. Which stairway? Was it E, or B, and which side? I cursed myself for being so stupid, but was somewhat consoled to note that I was not the only one to have become disorientated after twenty-four hours afloat. Eventually I located the group of bikers, who apparently had experienced no difficulty finding their way down — which made me feel even more stupid — and were again demonstrating warm camaraderie with handshakes and best wishes all round. Then a final check that panniers were securely attached and helmets properly fitted and we were ready for 'the off'. At last the huge doorway opened up and the ferry started to disgorge its contents. Bicycles led the way, quickly past passport control and out on to the road. This was it — we were on our way! The busy street leading out of the city was negotiated successfully, but we then got into deep trouble: the street led directly on to an *autopista* (motorway) with no obvious alternative. The toots of passing motorists spelled out quite clearly "get off the motorway you idiots". Get off we did, but not before taking some advantage of the situation by covering several miles as fast as we could, too preoccupied to admire the masses of tall silvery pampas grass plumes adorning the roadsides and worried that the motorway police might spot us — which would not have been a happy start to our trip. We then proceeded more leisurely and safely on an old road running roughly parallel to the *autopista;* we were later informed that there is a lane leading to this road just before joining the *autopista* in Santander.

A roadside bar offered the opportunity to recover from our dash on the motorway and to make our first contact with the natives. It was not to be a stimulating encounter. Our cheery greeting of *"buenos dias"* was barely acknowledged by the only man in the place, who was slumped over the bar, or by the woman behind it. I speak Spanish reasonably well and Roger thought he did, and we were eager to communicate. Having ordered drinks we asked if she could offer us something to eat. *"No"* was the simple reply, with no hint of regret or apology. This was unusual because, as we were to find, bars in Spain generally produce some food, if only a snack, at any time of the day. Spaniards, especially of the north, are sometimes described as surly and uncommunicative, and these two specimens seemed to fit that description. The *autopista* was completed only a few years ago and it is unlikely that many travellers now pass their way, so one might have expected some interest in the arrival of two elderly English gentlemen on bicycles. We tried to impress them by telling them of our aim to cycle to the south of the country, but this did not stir them. Clearly they were not interested in the *Viejo Equipo,* so we drank our beers and left.

From Torrelavega (about 25km from Santander) the main road south (N611) continues as a single carriageway, but, much to our surprise and delight, with a good 'hard shoulder', not as wide as on the *autopista* but generous enough for bicyles and other slow-moving vehicles. This was a luxury we had no reason to expect, but one we were to enjoy not only on all the major roads but also on some of the minor roads throughout our trip. The road cuts through two steep-sided gorges, running just above the Rio Besayo, before breaking out into more open farming country. There, about 30km south of Torrelavega, the road passes the small village of Helguera, too small to be marked on my map. In need of refreshment we turned in, hoping to find a bar. We were in luck: the Bar Miguel was just a few hundred yards from the main road. There we met two young men, probably in their early 30s, and the next hour or so served to establish our relationship with Spaniards at a proper level. Their names were Eduardo and Fernando and they helped run their family farms close by. They had not met many Englishmen. They were surprised to hear that we had cycled from Santander, and amazed that we were heading for the south coast.

"*Porque?*" (why?) Eduardo asked.

"Because we want to see if we can do it", I explained.

"*Mas tranquilo en coche*" (easier by car), he said.

Conversation became progressively easier as beer followed beer. Fernando kept saying he was going fishing but kept staying for one more. By that stage we were hoping there was a *hostal* in the village, but there was not. However, we were told that accommodation could be found in Barcena de Pié de Concha, the next village just 5km down the road. We said goodbye to our friends, who said they hoped we would meet many friendly Spaniards on our way. (We agreed but felt that if they all drink as much as these two we would have trouble reaching our destination.) Before reaching the main road we realised that we had left our helmets behind. Returning, we met Eduardo and Fernando running down the road, helmets held aloft.

Barcena de Pié de Concha is a pleasant little village nestling in the foothills of the Cordillera Cantabrica, the range of mountains that runs east-west across northwest Spain. The houses, with exposed timbers and wooden balconies, are typical of those in the northern provinces but quite different from those we were to see anywhere south of the *cordillera*. There were three bar/restaurants around the small square next to the river; we went to the Bar Miguel which Eduardo and Fernando had recommended. There we met Maite, who runs the place almost single-handedly because her husband has a part-time job and is away several days every week. She is a plain, thin, energetic young lady in her early 30s, and she could not have been more friendly and obliging; so much so that when she brought us a pork stew for dinner after we had both ordered duck (she had even confirmed our choice by cackling "quack-quack" and flapping her arms) we

Barcena de Pié de Concha

had to smile and say how wonderful her duck was. When, next morning, we were charged 2400 pesetas (£10) for dinner, bed and breakfast, we were more than satisfied.

CHAPTER 2
CROSSING THE CORDILLERA

BARCENA TO

HERRERA DE PISUERGA

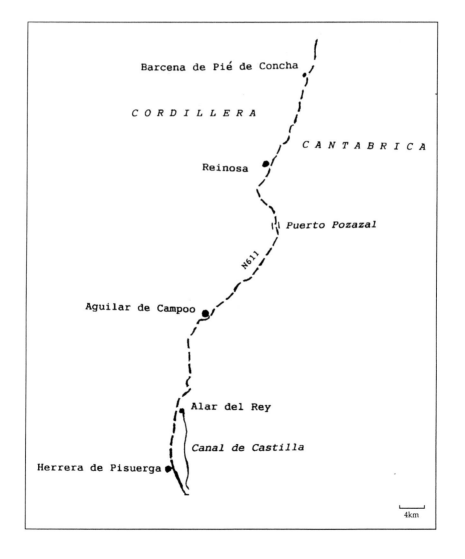

The road immediately climbs out of Barcena and continues fairly steeply for about 7km, up a narrow gorge with the river below. The gradient was such that stronger legs than mine would have been required to cycle up it, so I was forced for the first time to dismount and push the bike. This gave me more time to admire the scenery but, because there was fairly heavy traffic and the road through the gorge is not wide enough to provide a hard shoulder, it was not an enjoyable walk. To make me feel worse, when I met Roger at the top (he had gone on ahead) he casually stated that he had cycled most of the way. This was hard to believe but I had to accept it and concede, rather reluctantly, that he had earned the King of the Mountains crown and could already claim the *maillot jaune*.

The Cordillera Cantabrica, which extends for nearly 200km across the north-west of Spain, has tended to isolate the northern provinces of Galicia, Asturias and Cantabria from the rest of Spain and to strengthen their sense of independence, which persists to the present day. The mountains formed an effective barrier against the Moors, who took only 7 years to overrun Spain after invading in AD711 but did not subdue the northern provinces. The peaks are highest in the west, many rising to over 8000ft; south of Santander the highest are about 5600ft.

It was from these mountains, around the Picos de Europa west of Santander, that one of the great heroes of Spanish history emerged to defy the Moors. His name was Pelayo, and in 722 (or thereabouts — the precise date in uncertain) he led a small band of resistance fighters to victory over an army of Moors at Covadonga, on the northern slopes of the Picos. Although Christian chroniclers claimed that the Moorish army was some 30,000 strong, historians consider that it was probably little more than an expeditionary force. However, the importance of the battle lies not with military details but with its religious significance. It is said that Pelayo faced the enemy holding high a wooden cross in one hand and his sword in another, and that the Virgin Mary made a miraculous appearance on the battle field. His victory was seen as a victory for Christianity over Islam and it inspired the Christians in their crusade of *reconquista*, which was pursued slowly but inexorably until the final overthrow of

Granada by Fernando and Isabel, the 'Catholic Monarchs', in January 1492. A shrine in a cave in Covadonga, which is said to have been a refuge for Pelayo, now holds his tomb and an image of the Virgin, and attracts a steady flow of committed pilgrims and curious tourists.

After the initial steep ascent from Barcena we climbed more steadily to the Puerto Pozazal (3237ft), 13km south of Reinosa, before reaching the undulating and increasingly flat terrain of the Castilian *meseta*. The *meseta* — from the Spanish *mesa* (table) — is the vast tableland that occupies the central part of the Iberian peninsula, extending from the Cantabrian mountains in the north to the Sierra Morena in the south, and from the Portuguese border in the west to the mountains of the Sistema Iberica well beyond Madrid in the east. It includes the autonomous regions of Castilla y León, which we had now entered, and Extremadura and Castilla-La Mancha further south. The kingdoms of Castilla and León were first united in 1037 when Fernando I of Castilla defeated Bermundo III of León near Carrion de los Condes and then married Bermundo's sister Sancha; it may not have functioned as a single unit continuously since that time, but today it is probably the largest autonomous region in Europe, covering over 94,000 sq. km. Judging by the graffiti on some road signs there are some people in León who would prefer it otherwise.

Nineteen kilometers south of Aquilar de Campoo is Alar del Rey, a small town at the head of the Canal de Castilla, which we were to meet at several points during the next two days. Just off the main road, and directed by a sign *Nacimiento del Canal de Castilla*, we came to a small monument where the canal meets the Rio Pisuerga, almost under the railway line that replaced the canal as a means of transport. About a hundred yards away original stone warehouses stand on one bank and, on the other, old cellars where the prisoners who built the canal were locked up for the night. The canal runs an inverted-Y course south from Alar del Rey, branching north of Palencia where one arm, the Canal de Campos, runs south-west to Medina de Rioseco and the other continues south to the city of Valladolid. Along its 207km it has 49 locks, some of which once generated power that operated

15

flour and paper mills, foundries, tanneries and other industries along its banks. Work started on the canal in 1753, but shortage of funds and interruptions caused by the Napoleonic and Carlist wars delayed its completion. The northern section and the Canal de Campos were used to some extent as early as 1804 but it was after its completion in 1849 that it became a busy waterway linking the centre of Castile with the north, facilitating transport of goods to and from the port of Santander. This, however, was short-lived, as its decline began in the 1860s with the arrival of the railways. It is now used only for the very important purpose of irrigation of the extensive agricultural lands of Castilla y León.

South of Alar del Rey we saw for the first time plantations of poplar trees, and their slender shape and limey-green spring foliage became a pleasant feature in the otherwise rather bare landscape during the next couple of days. The trees (known in Spain as *chopos*) produce soft, poor-quality wood which, nevertheless, has many uses; for example, it is used extensively to make crates for transporting fruit and vegetables..

By the time we reached the small town of Herrera de Pisuerga, 75km from Barcena, we were feeling very tired and we staggered into the first bar we encountered. My legs felt as if they were filled with lead, and the front of my thighs ached so much that it was difficult to stand up after sitting down. And this was just the second day — how would they feel on the following day, and the one after that, I wondered? Roger complained of soreness in delicate areas between his legs. He felt he needed some protective padding and came up with the ingenious idea that sanitary towels might be employed to good effect — but he did not test this because he could not quite summon the nerve to ask the attractive young lady assistant at the pharmacy across the street.

We walked around the small but impressive *plaza mayor*, which is lined with some fine houses bearing the arms of noble families, and had a drink in the only bar, surprisingly named Covent Garden. At the top end of the *plaza* stand the remains of old Moorish walls.

We were directed to the Hotel Rigo. It was hardly a hotel, just a bar/restaurant with basic accommodation above, but good value at 3000 pesetas (£12) for a double room. The bar was typical of many we were to see on our journey: a room lacking any sense of decor, furnished only with a few wooden chairs and tables scattered on a tiled floor, and a television set mounted high on a bare wall; the clientele exclusively male, playing cards or watching television (either football or a bullfight), almost all of them smoking, their loud voices reverberating around the room, competing with the television commentary; fag-ends, paper napkins, peanut husks and other assorted debris ankle-deep on the floor; not the classiest of establishments but a popular meeting place (for the male of the species at least). Certainly this was a popular bar — a football match featuring Barcelona and Atletico Madrid was, no doubt, an added attraction. Later, after resting aching muscles for a couple of hours and returning to the bar, the attraction was a bullfight.

People have strong and widely disparate opinions about bullfighting: some see it as a supreme exhibition of courage, skill and artistry, and others as an example of barbaric cruelty to animals. It cannot be denied that a *corrida* is a magnificent spectacle. The *toreros*, resplendent in their fine, brightly-coloured suits, march into the ring to applause from an expectant crowd and to the strains of a *pasodoble*; a bugle call announces the imminent entry of the bull; the ferocious animal, specially bred for the ring, charges in to roars of the crowd, attacks the perimeter barrier and is then faced by the matador waving a large cape. Several distinct stages of the ritual then follow, each introduced by a bugle call: the *picador* on horseback thrusts a long sharp lance several times into the neck and shoulder of the charging bull; *banderilleros* on foot skilfully plant long darts into the wounded neck; finally the matador works with a smaller red cape, the *muleta*, dicing with death as the bull brushes past him time and again, his bravery and technique greeted with chants of "*olé*", the crowd tense as well as excited, aware that a moment of carelessness or excessive bravado could cost the matador his life. The drama eventually reaches its climax with a thrust of the matador's sword. A magnificent spectacle it might be, but most non-Spaniards cannot watch it without experiencing at least some moments of distress, or even of revulsion. Henry James wrote, in

17

his *Collected Travel Writings: The Continent (1876)*, that "a bullfight will, to a certain extent, bear looking at, but it will not bear thinking of", and Kate O'Brien in *Farewell Spain* concluded that "either it gets you or you're sick". Most northern Europeans are indeed sickened by bullfighting and would like to see it banned, but most Spaniards see it as part of their culture and, as such, never to be abandoned.

As a teenager returning on holiday to my home in Gibraltar I more than once visited the annual *feria* in La Linea, the Spanish border town. The *feria* in a small town like La Linea cannot be compared with that in, for example, Seville, but nevertheless it generates excitement and fun for a whole week and the festivities include a series of bullfights. I marvelled at the bravery and artistry of great matadors like Antonio Bienvenida, Domingo Ortega and, especially, Luis Miguel Dominguin, and also at the superb horsemanship of Angel Peralta fighting bulls on horseback, but the names I remember best are Miguel Baez Litri, Julio Aparicio and Antonio Ordoñez, three outstanding *novilleros* who regularly featured on the same bill. Despite not being fully-fledged matadors and therefore fighting smaller bulls, their brilliance captivated the crowds and attracted at least as many *aficionados* as did the great matadors of the day. I have not attended a bullfight since those days nearly 50 years ago (nor have I wanted to) but here in the bar at Herrera de Pisuerga the memories came flooding back as I watched, to my surprise, another Litri in action — Litri's son, I was told. I later discovered that a son of Julio Aparicio and a nephew of Antonio Ordoñez are also matadors today.

CHAPTER 3
THE CASTILIAN *CAMPO*
Herrera to Villarramiél

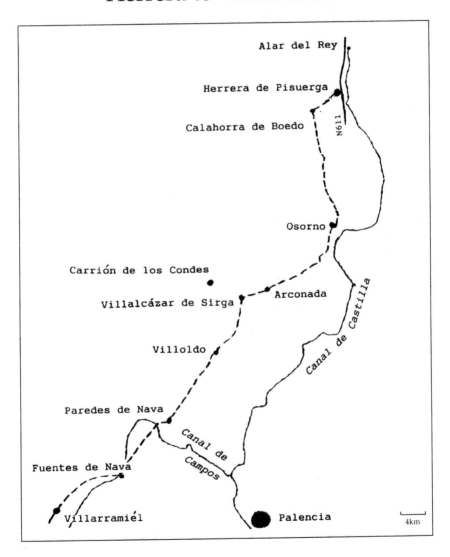

The next day the old legs still felt so stiff that a great effort was required to lift one up sufficiently to mount the bicycle — it seemed doubtful that they could respond to the demands of another day's pedalling. However, we set off cross-country, away from the main N611 for the first time, and made good progress along traffic-free roads across mostly flat agricultural land, through or past numerous small towns or villages — Calahorra de Boedo, Osorno, Villalcázar de Sirga, Villoldo, Paredes de Nava, Fuentes de Nava — before ending up after nearly 100km in Villarramiél.

At Villalcázar de Sirga our route crossed the Camino de Santiago, the famous pilgrimage route that runs from four main starting points in France south and then westwards for about 1600km to the shrine of the apostle St James (Santiago in Spanish) in Santiago de Compostela. Thousands of people have been making the pilgrimage since Alfonso II of Asturias built a shrine on the spot where, in AD813, a late-Roman tomb was discovered on a hillside and was claimed to contain Santiago's remains. The basis for this claim is at best tenuous. There is no firm evidence that Santiago spent any time in Spain — it is not even recorded in the Bible. It is known that he was beheaded in Jerusalem in AD44, but it is hardly credible that his body should have been removed by his followers, taken all the way to Spain by boat along the whole length of the Mediterranean and up the Atlantic coast (in four days according to the legend), buried in Galicia, discovered more than 700 years later by a peasant who was attracted to the hill by a vision of stars (thus the name Compostela), and identified by a local bishop as Santiago. However, such is the stuff of legends, and Santiago was soon adopted by Spaniards as their patron saint in their defiance of the Moors (who at that time controlled all except that northwestern region of Spain), and became their inspiration during the protracted but eventual reconquest of their country for Christianity, during which he was also named Santiago Matamoros (Moor killer). Pilgrims, many of them French, were soon flocking to the shrine — it has been reported that during the 11th and 12th centuries more than 500,000 made the pilgrimage every year. Nowadays the numbers are less staggering: the official register in Santiago de Compostela recorded the arrival of 25,179 pilgrims in 1997, many, no doubt, having walked or cycled the famous route for recreational rather than religious reasons. Monasteries, churches, hospitals and other important buildings sprouted up all along the route, many exhibiting the Romanesque style of architecture that prevailed throughout western Europe between the 10th and 13th centuries, as well as the later Gothic. In Villalcázar de Sirga, which is only a small town, there is the Hermitage of Nuestra Señora del Rio and the church of Santa Maria la Blanca, the latter standing at the top of wide flights of stone steps, its size and position dwarfing and dominating all around it.

Villarramiél is a small town with a simple but pleasant *plaza mayor* that boasts a central bandstand and is bordered by pollarded plane trees, its top branches at a level of about 8ft pulled out horizontally and intertwined with branches from neighbouring trees — during the hot summer months this arrangement must provide a welcome canopy. The *plaza* was deserted, but the first bar we entered was alive with men playing cards or dominoes.

Plaza Mayor, Villarramiél

21

We were told that another bar on the *plaza*, the Bar Tercio, offered accommodation. This was a larger bar, also well patronized, again by men only. We were told that most of the men of the town worked in the *campo*, but since at least two bars in town were now full of them, it was clear that Saturday afternoon was a time for relaxation, not work.

We were offered a comfortable room overlooking the *plaza*. After a hot bath and a rest we were back in the bar and, to our surprise, the scene was entirely different. At several of the tables were now seated smartly dressed ladies, and their menfolk were socializing with them, not playing cards or watching the football match being shown on television. We suspected that to be taken out to the Bar Tercio was the ladies' weekend treat and that the men were on their best behaviour to ensure that they were let out on their own every other evening of the week.

The bar was now being run by the owner's teenage son and daughter, who were clearly taking their responsibilities seriously. The youngsters, like others we met on our journey, were keen to practise their English. "What is your name?", "How old are you?", "Two beers, three hundred pesetas". I asked a man at the bar about life and work in the *campo*; he painted a picture of long hours and hard graft but, he assured us, despite life's hardships, Spaniards are always *"alegre"* (cheerful) — a nice thought, so I didn't tell him that we had already met exceptions to this. Unfortunately, nowhere is there a Utopia where everyone is always cheerful — everywhere there are cheerful souls and miserable sods, the proportion of each varying both within and between countries.

The Bar Tercio did not offer food, so a bar round the corner was recommended. There we first encountered *platos combinados*. In general, Spaniards, like the French, do not load different types of food on a plate. Whereas in Britain it would not be unusual to be given meat or fish accompanied by three or four vegetables, in Spain or France it is usually a few chips and nothing else. But *platos combinados* are different: they include any combination of eggs, sausages, steak, ham, bacon, tomatoes, mushrooms, chips, and more — a huge fry-up, in other words. After a long day in the saddle this sort of food, washed down with a bottle of wine, however rough, is more satisfying than exquisitely prepared *nouvelle cuisine*. We were the only diners, the others standing at the bar (as is their custom) adding to the already considerable litter on the floor, watching the obligatory football match on television or playing a fruit machine. The noise and flashing lights of these abominable machines are to be found in every Spanish bar — I doubt if there is a bar anywhere in Spain that does not have at least one of these monsters.

It was reassuring to note that my legs, which had seemed at the beginning of the day unlikely to take me very far, had propelled me a further 96km without undue trouble — they seemed to be warming to their task. However, muscles forced to push pedals round and round all day seem to complain when then asked to move legs alternately one in front of the other (especially going up stairs) or to lift a body up from a seated to a standing position. These activities continued to cause great discomfort, especially at the front of the thighs, and anyone witnessing my progress up even a short flight of stairs would not have given much for my chances of going much further on this trip.

It was a wet *plaza* that I looked down upon next morning. As our bar was not due to open until mid-morning we crossed to the bar across the *plaza*. We had by this stage already discovered that breakfast in a Spanish café of bar is rather basic: usually just coffee and toast (*tostada*). Popular alternatives appear to be hot chocolate instead of coffee and a *madalena* (sweet bun) instead of toast. Almost always available is *zumo de naranja* (orange juice) squeezed to order at the bar from fresh oranges — we were never given orange juice from a carton. Coffee is invariably of the expresso type and is served in standard measures: either *café solo* (black, served in a tiny cup), or *café con leche* (nearly half milk, in a large cup), or *café cortado* (less milk, but served in a smaller cup). My taste is for *café cortado* but in a large cup, for which it was necessary to specify *doble* or *grande*. The *tostada* is normally a large bread roll cut in half rather than a slice of bread, and the butter (*mantequilla*) and jam (*mermelada*) are usually provided in those ubiquitous small plastic containers that have found their way to dining tables around the world. *Mermelada* is rarely what we in Britain call marmalade but, most commonly, strawberry or apricot jam. This light breakfast did not seem ideal for providing the calories necessary for a hard day on the road but it had to do.

Returning to the Bar Tercio we found that the daily cleaning lady had been hard at work. There was no sign of the assorted debris that covered the floor the previous evening — the whole place was spotlessly and sparklingly clean. This was something else we were discovering about Spanish bars: whatever mess is made during the day it is all gone by opening time next morning. Customers clearly feel no need to be concerned about littering the floor because they know that someone will clear it up in the morning. Why bother to look for ashtrays and litter bins when fag-ends and other rubbish can simply be dropped on the floor?

CHAPTER 4
THE RAIN IN SPAIN . . .
VILLARRAMIÉL TO TORO

We set out from Villarramiél rather reluctantly in light rain. However, it did seem appropriate that, as the song goes, rain should be falling on the plain as we headed south-west towards Toro. We were on quiet country roads, crossing land intensely cultivated with cereal and vegetable crops, which were difficult to identify in their early spring growth. Across the flat landscape isolated villages stood out far away on the skyline, each dominated by a solid, austere church (many having at some time served as refuge and fortress as well as church), and a water tower, surprisingly elegant brick structures with sloping orange tiled roofs. The rain was persistent but not heavy and we found it pleasantly refreshing, the whizzing of tyres as they splashed through puddles evoking memories of simple childhood pleasures.

The road passing through the small city of Medina de Rioseco skirts round the old quarter, but a short diversion into the centre was very rewarding: an impressive main street leading to a fine *plaza mayor*; remains of old city walls with three gateways, one dating from the 13th century; and no less than six churches or convents dating from the 16th and 17th centuries. It is not surprising that the city is officially designated as a place of special historical and artistic interest. The buildings provide an excellent choice of nesting sites for white storks, which we saw here for the first time but which were to be a feature of the landscape for most of our journey. The Calle Lázaro Alonso, the main street, only 12 to 15 feet wide, is impressive because of its colonnaded and arcaded pavements on each side, each arcade almost as wide as the street itself and sheltering some surprisingly stylish shops. Many of the oldest columns, of wood and stone, are still standing, but some have been replaced by less impressive concrete columns. Clearly it was a rich and important city in its time; it was granted city status by Felipe IV in 1632. It is at the centre of the Tierra de Campos, the vast agricultural lands of Castilla y León, and it is also at the southern limit of the Canal de Campos, the south-western arm of the Canal de Castilla, the northern end of which we saw in Alar del Rey. Here the canal is widened into a U-shaped basin, flanked by granaries and warehouses and bordered by a sadly unkempt garden, the Jardines de Concha, con-

26

Calle Lázaro Alonso, Medina de Rioseco

The southern end of the Canal de Campos, Medina de Rioseco

taining poplars, silver birch, lilacs and an avenue of pollarded plane trees.

Heading south-west out of Medina de Rioseco (which, of course, means 'city of the dry river') we soon crossed the river that runs through it. It is called the Sequillo, which means 'dryish', and this, we had been told, is more accurate than the name of the city implies because the river is rarely *seco*; it has occasionally even been known to flood, but it is usually *sequillo*. We passed more poplar plantations, and storks nesting on electricity pylons (presumably finding it too crowded in the city) before riding through a grand archway topped with a clock tower and past an impressive church in an otherwise rather delapidated Villabrágima, a town that in the middle ages had a large Jewish population and was an important commercial centre.

We had been urged to visit Urueña, a few kilometers off our route. The climb to the hilltop village was well worth the effort. Riding through a gateway in the old walls that encircle the village we found ourselves in an environment that can have changed little since medieval times. Narrow streets pass between ancient stone buildings, some of which have finally succumbed to the elements, and lead at the far end of the village to another gateway beyond which there is a sheer drop to the valley below. The village was almost deserted; we saw no bars or cafés or even shops, except, surprisingly, a bookshop, which seemed totally out of place there. From a path high on the wall there is a bird's eye view of tightly-packed tiled rooftops and of the vast flat plain stretching far into the distance.

Shortly after passing under the NVI *autovia* we came upon a roadside bar, the Bar Los Angeles, on entering the village of Tiedra. There were only a few men in the bar, but the place remains memorable because of the amazing volume of noise they managed to generate, not by singing or fighting or throwing furniture about but simply by talking. Spaniards are reputed to talk louder than most other people, but these hardy souls of Tiedra surpassed anything that might reasonably be expected. Their voices filled the room, reverberating and echoing, individual voices lost in the overall cacophony. Roger and I, sitting aside and marvelling at their prowess, attempted to emulate them but,

Urueña — gateway

Urueña — walls and rooftops

like new musicians joining a band, we would have needed some practice before striking the right volume and pitch.

We were soon on the road again, our ears ringing, passing a tiny 13th-century castle perched on a mound by the road out of Tiedra. We reached Toro in mid-afternoon. Entering the town through the Arco de Corredera, then under the ornate Torre del Reloj (clock tower), we reached the Plaza Mayor, quiet as usual in mid-afternoon except for storks clattering on the rooftops. After a short rest with a cool drink stork-watching in the *plaza*, Roger was keen to hit the road again, but I managed to restrain him. Beyond the *plaza* the cobbled street runs past the impressive Colegiata de Santa Maria la Mayor and then opens out suddenly into the Plaza Espolón and to a magnificent panorama beyond. From the edge of this *plaza* there is a sheer drop of about 300 feet to the flat plain below, the Rio Duero coming in from the south and taking a right-angle turn to the west under a Roman bridge and over a weir. The Rio Duero is one of the four great Spanish rivers that flow out to the Atlantic, part of its course forming the border between Spain and Portugal. On one side of the Plaza

Rio Duero turning west at Toro

31

Colegiata de Santa Maria, Toro

Espolón stands the Colegiata and on the other the Hotel Juan II, named after a king of Castile, father of Isabel who was to become Queen of Castile in 1478. The hotel looked rather 'up-market' compared to the modest establishments we had lodged in so far, but this appealed to Roger, who enjoys his creature comforts. I was concerned that his appearance — bright yellow top, turquoise shorts, dirty shoes, blue helmet and dark eyeshades — might hinder our chances of being offered a room. I was dressed more conservatively, so I suggested that I should be the one to approach the receptionist and that he should stay out of sight outside. He would have none of it, confident that his natural charm would prevail. The fact that the hotel was almost empty probably had a greater influence on the outcome, and we were shown to one of their best rooms at a corner of the building, with views on one side to the Colegiata across the Plaza Espolón and on the other over the wonderful panorama to the south.

A routine had by now become established. Having reached a suitable destination by mid- or late afternoon, the first priority was to start the revitalization process by consuming a few beers, then to arrange overnight accommodation, then to assume a horizontal position either on a bed or in a bath, or both in random order, and sleep for a period of time dependent on the toll taken by the day's exertions. At least partly restored, shirt, socks and underpants had to be washed and hung out to dry on a window or balcony. Chores completed we would set out to explore the town, if it was not already late enough for pangs of hunger to send us immediately in search of food. Having arrived fairly early in Toro there was time to visit the Colegiata and admire its 13th-century west portal, recognized as an outstanding example of Romanesque art, before strolling around the old streets. We noticed that many of the buildings are faced with unusual brickwork: the bricks are thinner than our standard house brick and are separated by an almost equal thickness of off-white mortar. The effect is certainly attractive. Later in our travels we were to see many types of building displaying this brickwork — not only houses but churches and church towers — and we learned that this is a style characteristic of Mudéjar architecture. Moors who stayed on after the Christians had driven their leaders out became known as Mudéjars, and many were skilled craftsmen who continued to work in their traditional ways. Their style has remained popular to the present day, being reflected in many modern buildings, including the Hotel Juan II.

Returning to the hotel, the large bar was now full of people, but instead of the motley crowd of men we had come to expect to find in a bar there were smartly-dressed family groups. It was a Sunday evening, and clearly the Hotel Juan II is a popular place for a family night out in Toro. Children, parents, grandparents, uncles, aunts: they were all there, loud babbles of conversation filling the room in best Spanish style. People-watching in a foreign country is an interesting and enlightening pastime. Here we were struck by the number of people smoking, an observation that was to be reinforced throughout our journey. News of the weed's health hazard has either hardly reached Spain or it is largely ignored, not only by the younger generation (who can be expected to ignore all advice because they always know best) but also by their supposedly more sensible but more addicted elders, women adopting the classic Lauren Bacall-type pose (cigarette in hand held high and tilted sharply back at the wrist) that years ago was considered rather sophisticated — and in Spain probably still is.

It is good to see extended families enjoying each other's company — a sight much more common in Mediterranean countries than in northern Europe — but I have to admit that I can do without young children running about in bars and restaurants in the evening (at any time, to be honest, but especially in the evening). When are young children put to bed in Spain? Much too late, it seems, because they can be seen and heard well into the evening. Do Spanish parents never seek respite during the day from their little darlings? Here a few young tearaways were having a grand time hurling themselves on to the highly polished marble floor, sliding from one end to the other, forcing long-suffering waiters holding trays of drinks aloft to take evasive action, while their parents looked on admiringly. We could stand it no more and headed for town.

It was still only about 7.30pm and restaurants had not yet opened. This can be a problem for northern Europeans in Spain:

few restaurants open for dinner before 8.00pm, many not before 8.30 or even 9.00pm. Even at 9.00pm dinner can be a solitary experience, the advantage of personal service hardly making up for the lack of ambience. Even Roger's stimulating conversation could not reasonably be expected to provide diversion and entertainment throughout a long evening. The alternative is to eat *tapas* or the larger-portion *raciónes* in a bar. Here we indulged in a bar crawl, which is particularly easy in Toro because of the many bars around the *plaza mayor* — in fact the east side of the *plaza* is an almost uninterrupted line of them.

Many Spanish bars, especially in towns, are simply long, narrow rooms, not much more than a wide corridor, the actual bar running along one side and occupying about half the space. Sometimes one or two tables and chairs are provided, but most customers seem to prefer to stand, probably to get the best view of the TV and the inevitable football match. On this busy night in Toro, customers were standing shoulder to shoulder. Most bars display a list of their *tapas/raciónes* on a blackboard behind the bar, but they also present a selection for inspection in glass cabinets on the bar. To examine them we had first to edge through the crowd and then, having reached the bar, to identify them. Some, like prawns, sardines, meat balls, egg mayonnaise or potato omelette, are quite easy to identify, but others may not be and could turn out to be congealed pig's blood or cocks' combs or sheep's testicles, so close inspection and identification are essential. Immediate payment is never requested, so another push through the crowd is needed in order to pay. Somehow the barmen (and they are almost invariably men, not women) manage to keep tabs on each customer even in the most crowded bar — only occasionally do they have to rely on customers telling them what they have had.

After visiting five or six bars and having a beer or a glass of wine with a *tapa* or *ración* in each we returned to the hotel feeling replete and relaxed. Moonlight shone on the tranquil plain, the Duero a long silver thread glistening in the darkness. It was hard to imagine that there, on a less peaceful day in 1476, an important battle took place.

On the death in 1474 of Enrique IV of Castilla (the son of Juan

II and his first wife Maria of Aragon) the succession was hotly disputed between Enrique's half-sister Isabel (whose mother was Juan II's second wife, Isabel of Portugal) and his daughter Juana. It was generally rumoured, however, that Juana was illegitimate (she is widely recorded in history as Juana la Beltranája, after the courtier Beltrán de la Cueva who was suspected of being her father), and Isabel therefore considered herself the rightful heiress. During his lifetime Enrique had not consistently supported the claim of one or the other, so the dispute inevitably led to civil war. Isabel had the support of Fernando of Aragon, whom he married in 1469, and Juana the support of Alfonso V of Portugal. Although the civil war lasted about 5 years after Enrique's death, Isabel and Fernando's victory at Toro was crucial in securing for Isabel the throne of Castile. Isabel and Fernando, always referred to as Los Reyes Catolicos (the Catholic Monarchs) in recognition of their profound catholicism, went on, of course, to have a huge influence on events throughout Spain, notably by their relentless pursuit of the Moors and ultimate success in driving them out of Spain in 1492, and their enthusiastic encouragement of the infamous Inquisition.

Another battle was to be waged that night in our hotel room. Roger and I were experienced room-mates — we had shared a room for 3 years as students in London with minimal conflict (I may have complained occasionally about noxious odours emanating from his feet) — and the first three nights on this trip in shared rooms passed peacefully enough. On this night in Toro, however, all was to change. I was accused of snoring, which, I admit, is extremely antisocial nocturnal behaviour, and his response was positively vicious. He drew the little table between the two beds towards his and then, with a firm and decisive action, drove it hard and fast against my bed, like an angry goat butting a rival. The effect was immediate, not only in stopping the snoring (albeit temporarily) but also in propelling me what felt like a few feet skywards. This violent attack was repeated at frequent intervals throughout the night after which we vowed, for different reasons, never to share a room again.

CHAPTER 5
THE ENDLESS PLAIN
TORO TO SALAMANCA

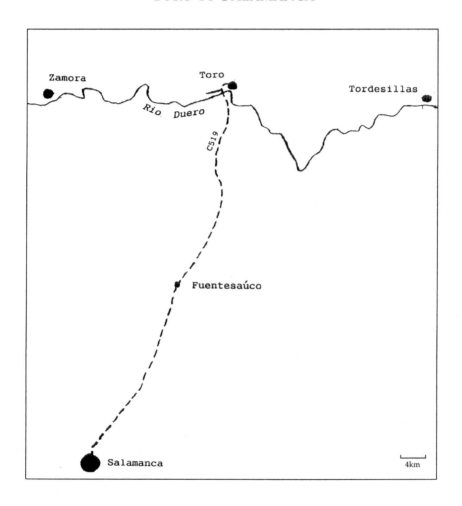

Highly recommended reading for anyone planning a journey in Spain is Laurie Lee's famous book *As I Walked Out One Midsummer Morning*, which describes his walk from Vigo in Galicia, where he arrived from London by ship in July 1935, to Andalucía in the south. His route crossed ours only at Toro, which he described, as he first saw it from the west, as an "eroded, red-walled town spread along the top of a huge flat boulder". This is the view we had on looking back at the town after descending the hill to the west on the Zamora road and crossing the river, the flat plain ending abruptly at the sheer face of red rock, the outline of the Colegiata dominating the skyline above the town.

With the town hardly out of sight I noticed that my front tyre had punctured. Roger was almost out of sight but just within earshot; I'm glad he was, because I would have had the greatest difficulty dealing with the problem by myself. For a 'real' cyclist, replacing a punctured inner tube is a routine and simple task; for me it would have been a major operation at the best of times, but on this occasion it may have been beyond me because I was handicapped by a mysterious injury. It involved almost total loss

Toro — the view described by Laurie Lee

of function of both my thumbs and it remains mysterious because I have yet to meet or hear of another cyclist who has suffered the same injury. The first sign was inability to exert the gentle pressure required to move the thumb-operated gear levers mounted on the handlebars; I overcame this difficulty by bending my thumbs and pushing with the knuckles. I also had to find alternative methods for such ordinary tasks as grasping a knife firmly enough to cut food or even squeezing toothpaste out of a tube. I can only suppose it was a type of repetitive stress injury (such as typists, for example, have been known to experience) caused by repetitive use of the thumbs when changing gear, but for this to have occurred after only four days was very hard to believe. It was at least two months after the end of our trip before normal function returned. Fortunately this was the only injury either of us suffered (aching thighs and numb backsides not being classified as injuries), and the puncture was the only problem we had with either of our bikes throughout the trip.

We continued on the quiet C519 all the way to Salamanca, an easy ride of 74km across farmland intensely cultivated with cereals, vegetables, sunflowers (not yet in flower), beet and also, close to Toro, vines. The vineyards stretch south of the Duero from Zamora, 33km to the west of Toro, to Tordesillas 37km to the east, and beyond to the Rueda district south of Valladolid. These vineyards are less well known internationally than those of Rioja, Penedés or Valdepeñas, but they contribute to the vast acreage of vineyards in Spain which, surprisingly, is greater than in France, Italy or Germany.

Mention of Tordesillas cannot pass without noting its important place in world history. The Treaty of Tordesillas, signed in 1494 with the authority of Pope Alexander VI, divided the New World in the west (the lands recently discovered and any others yet to be discovered) between Spain and Portugal, resulting in most of the Americas going to Spain and Brazil to Portugal. The town is also well known as the place that Juana la Loca (Joan the Mad)) was confined for 46 years. Daughter of Isabel and Fernando, she became queen of Castile on the death of her brother, and married Felipe I (Philip the Handsome) of Austria. She was so enamoured with him that when he died in 1506 she travelled through Castile for 3 years with his body in an open coffin. After she arrived in Tordesillas in 1504 her father and later her brother (Carlos V) declared her insane. Felipe's body was taken for burial in Burgos and Juana was confined in the Real Monasterio de Santa Clara.

We stopped for lunch half way between Toro and Salamanca, in Fuentesaúco. Not recognizing the *tapas* displayed on the bar I pointed to each in turn and asked the barman to identify them. The first was *lengua* (tongue), the next *orejas* (ears), and the next *morro* (snout), all of pigs. I stopped him at that point: both of us were usually game to try something new but neither of us felt tempted by these particular delicacies. We settled for cheese *bocadillos* and agreed to his suggestion that he should add tomato to them. (A *bocadillo* is a large sandwich usually made with a generous section of a *baguette*-type loaf.) When they were brought to us we found the only signs of tomato were a few pips under the cheese. When I asked what had happened to the tomato he explained (clearly surprised by the question) that the bread had been *"refregado con tomate"* (rubbed with tomato). We were certainly learning a thing or two in this bar. But why rub with tomato instead of inserting slices in the *bocadillo*? We did not pursue the matter so the question remains unanswered. However, we had already found elsewhere that *bocadillos* are normally made without butter and therefore tend to be rather dry, so was rubbing with tomato supposed to improve it by contributing a little moisture as well as a subtle flavour? We remained puzzled. We ate many *bocadillos* during our trip but the Fuentesaúco variety seems to be unique.

As we rode out of Fuentesaúco we had our first confrontation with Spanish dogs. Several travellers in Spain, including Robin Neillands, have described hair-raising encounters with ferocious dogs, and these came flooding to mind as we approached three large dogs prowling the roadside. When they saw us they turned and moved slowly in our direction. Would they be friendly or would they go for our ankles? We slowed down, ready to dismount and defend ourselves (what with I don't know — we had no weapons, unlike Neillands who carried a stick especially to fend off dogs, and had to use it). The moment of truth was approaching. The dogs had their eyes fixed on us and we kept ours even more firmly fixed on them — which was to be our downfall, literally, because I ran into the back of Roger's bike and we both fell to the ground. The dogs, instead of seizing the opportunity to attack just stood there looking at us, no doubt puzzled and amused by our strange behaviour. Lying there on the ground we felt very foolish. The only fierce dogs we were to meet barked menacingly as we passed but were securely tied up or safely confined behind a fence.

I approached Salamanca with a sense of excitement at the prospect of visiting a beautiful city, but also with some trepidation. Up to this point on our trip we had avoided big cities, and the thought of busy streets choked with traffic was not appealing. However, my concern proved to be unfounded. Following directions to *centro ciudad*, we negotiated the Avenida de Mirat and the Paseo de las Carmelitas, which skirt the northern and western perimeter of the city centre, without difficulty. Stopping near a small roadside garden, the Campo de San Fernando, we were told that we were only a stone's throw from the Plaza Mayor. We pushed our bikes along narrow streets and then suddenly, walking through an archway, we entered the magnificent square. Its grandeur cannot fail to have an immediate and stunning impact on the senses. I felt like an actor must feel stepping out from the wings on to the stage of a grand theatre. It must be one of the most impressive *plazas* in Spain, the square itself (measuring about 80 x 90 yards) bare except for three equally-spaced stone benches on each side and a tall lamp-post supporting five elegant lamps in the centre, but completely enclosed by a magnificent four-storey building of golden sandstone, the ground floor housing shops and cafés sheltered by a colonnaded arcade. The *plaza*, which was completed in 1755, was the work of Andrea Garcia Quiñones and Alberto Churriguera; the latter was the younger brother of José, after whom the early 18th-century Churriqueresque style of architecture was named. We sat outside at one of the cafés in the afternoon sunshine, enjoying a few beers and marvelling at the wonderful scene. It is a traffic-free zone, pedestrians crossing to archways set in the middle of each side and at each corner, and it is, of course, the hub of the city.

Plaza Mayor, Salamanca

One of the most agreeable things about Spain is that almost every town, however modest, has a *plaza mayor* which is the focal point of its social life. Up to the end of the 18th century it was also where bullfights were staged, before separate bullrings were built. There are now some magnificent bullrings in Spain but perhaps none as grand as the *plaza mayor* in Salamanca.

Suitably refreshed, we set out in search of accommodation. We did not have far to go. The Calle de Meléndez, just off the south side of the Plaza Mayor, offers several *pensiónes*. We rang the bell of the first one (Pensión Lisboa) and were soon greeted by a squat, middle-aged man, Chaplin-like with a small moustache. Yes, he said, he had two rooms available (both of us now insisting on separate rooms), but no, he had nowhere to keep the bikes. (On our previous overnight stops this had not presented a problem.) After a pregnant pause, during which he must have visualized a few thousand pesetas passing him by, he relented and offered to keep the bicycles in his flat, which was on the second floor, the *pensión* rooms being on the third. (He told me later that he does not normally allow bikes into his flat but that he had

Salamanca — Rua Mayor and Catedral Nueva

made an exception in our case — he must have had a cash-flow problem at the time.) We struggled up the narrow staircase leading to his flat and were invited to park the bikes in his dining room. It was a tidy, well-furnished flat, and the bikes looked out of place resting against an antique sideboard amidst highly polished furniture and silverware. I wondered what his wife would have to say to him about it. Roger had a spacious room with *en suite* bathroom at the front of the building, from which next morning he was able to cast his eye over tne young ladies making their way to the university just down the road. I had a poky room at the back with an excellent view of a bare stone wall a few feet from my tiny window — I knew my place in our *equipo*.

The recuperation period here was shorter than on previous days, partly because the ride from Toro had not been too demanding, and partly because we were impatient to explore the city. A short walk down the pedestrianized Rua Mayor was rewarded with the delights of the huge Baroque church of La Clerica, the early 16th-century mansion Casa de las Conchas (House of Shells), its facades decorated with rows of sculptured scallop shells, several grand university buildings, the two cathedrals (the newer and larger Gothic Catédral Nueva and the Romanesque Catedral Vieja) standing side by side, sharing a common wall, and the Palacio de Anaya across a square from the cathedrals. Just a short distance away are the convents of Las Dueñas and San Esteban. The golden sandstone from which all these buildings (and, indeed all others in the old part of the city) were constructed greatly enhances their beauty and one can only feel extremely humble in their presence. Just beyond the cathedrals the Rio Tormes and the quarter-mile-long Roman bridge come into view.

Grand old buildings impart a sense of history and solidity to a city. In Salamanca this is tempered and given vitality by the presence of many universiy students. The university, which was founded in 1218 by Alfonso IX, is the oldest in Spain and for several centuries enjoyed an international reputation second to none. More recently its standing has fallen behind several other Spanish universities, but it still enrols about 12,000 students, among whom are many foreigners attending the popular language school. Although university students, in my experience, are prone from time to time to indulge in antisocial behaviour, much to the annoyance and even disgust of local residents, such behaviour tends to be reserved for late-evening revelry, and during the day they can appear quite civilised and contribute youthful colour to a city.

It was in Salamanca that I first noted Roger's obsession with the fax machine. It was, of course, highly desirable for us to communicate with our families back home, many of whom had expressed grave doubts about the wisdom of our trip and were anxious to be reassured that we were still alive or, at least, still in one piece. But whereas I fulfilled this responsibility quickly and simply by using a telephone, Roger was drawn inexorably towards that more modern wonder of technology. The problem was where to find one. Hotels seemed the most likely sort of place, but, having located one, it was then necessary to obtain the operator's co-operation. If the operator was female he turned on the charm, something he considered he was quite good at, even in his halting Spanish. To his surprise and annoyance this was not always successful and a determined search continued all over town. And this was not the only search. He was also a great writer of postcards, which need stamps, and to buy stamps in Spain it is necessary to look either for a post office (which may be difficult to find and, if found, is usually closed) or an *estanco*, a shop selling tobacco and newspapers. The abiding mental picture I have of Roger in a Spanish town is of him purposefully striding the streets looking for a fax machine or an *estanco* or both. I don't know when he found the mental energy to compose his fax and postcard messages — I guess it was while lying in a bath at the end of a day's cycling, a time when I was invariably dead to the world and incapable of the faintest spark mental energy. Roger was a man who could not remain idle, even while lying in a bath.

CHAPTER 6
A CHANGING LANDSCAPE
SALAMANCA TO BÉJAR

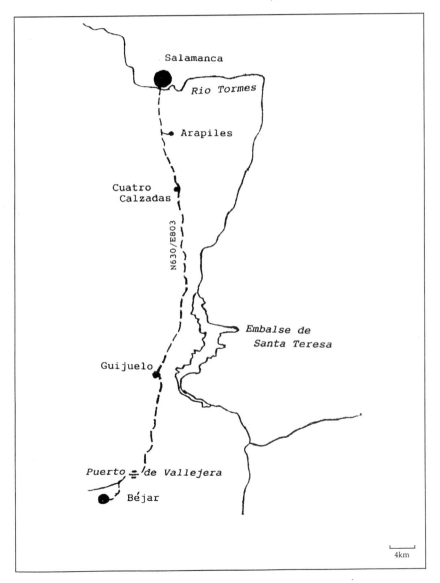

Next morning, which was cool and bright, we took a final stroll along the Rua Mayor and around the Plaza Mayor, absorbing again the grandeur of it all. (It has to be said, however, that Roger in his brightly-coloured cycling gear looked incongruous in the grand setting.) Later we rode out over the Puente de Enrique Estevan, managing to get a quick glimpse of the Roman bridge to our right, and then out on the main road south, the N630/E803, which we were to follow for the next two days. This was our first encounter with a main road since we left Herrera de Pisuerga on the third day. The country roads had been wonderfully free of traffic, but it was inevitable that it would be different on the main road. However, the road surface was excellent and a wide 'shoulder' provided a superb cycling track and safety from the passing traffic.

Just off the road a few miles south of Salamanca is the village of Arapiles where Sir Arthur Wellesley (later to become the Duke of Wellington) defeated the French in July 1812 in what is better known in Britain as the Battle of Salamanca. The French had invaded Spain in October 1807 and Napoleon had installed his brother, Joseph Bonaparte, as king. In 1808 Britain had come to support the already fierce Spanish guerilla resistance. Wellesley arrived in Lisbon with a fresh army in April 1809 (he had enjoyed some success the previous year before being recalled to Britain), fought a famous but inconclusive battle at Talavera, south-west of Madrid, in July 1809 before retreating to Portugal. After resisting a long French siege in Lisbon during 1810-1811, his decisive offensive got under way after capturing Ciudad Rodrigo in January 1812 and Badajoz in May 1812, and his victory at Arapiles on the 21st of July 1812 was the first of a series that finally drove the French across the Pyrenees. On an isolated rocky ridge outside the village stands a simple stone monument commemorating the battle. The owner of a local bar was apologetic about it, feeling that the event merited a much grander monument or, better still, that it should be celebrated by a week of *fiesta*.

The landscape south of Salamanca is quite different from that north of the city. Whereas to the north the flat plains are intensely cultivated, to the south the land soon turns to undulating

Monument commemorating the Battle of Salamanca (Arapiles)

49

grassland dotted with holm oaks (*encinas*). This type of land-scape was to dominate for many miles south, into Extremadura and the Sierra Morena. The oaks spread across the land as far as the eye can see. Here and there cattle and, especially, pigs, graze contentedly under the trees, the acorns an important source of food. We stopped for a drink at a roadside bar/restaurant at Cuatro Calzadas, where the road had risen to an altitude of 3770ft. Sitting in the small garden in the sunshine we enjoyed a panoramic view, especially to the south-east, where snow-covered peaks dominated a distant *sierra*. (I was pleased we were heading directly south.) We stopped again for refreshment in Guijelo, a centre for the manufacture of the cured pork products that are much loved in Spain. The beer-pump handles were moulded in the shape of large legs of pork, emphasizing that this was pig country.

As far as Salamanca I had managed to keep up with Roger (except, of course, on the climb up the Cordillera Cantabrica, when he was crowned King of the Mountains) but now, as the terrain became more undulating, I found it increasingly difficult. The gradients were not very steep but some, nevertheless, were quite demanding, and it was here that his prowess once again became apparent as he pulled away slowly but inexorably. Forever the competitor, he imagined himself racing in the *Tour de France*, making the decisive spurt to 'break the field' and head for victory. On reaching the top of an incline he would change gear, put his head down and pedal even harder down the slope on the other side so as to experience the sheer exhilaration of speed. I, on the other hand, would gasp for breath, stop pedalling and enjoy the luxury of free-wheeling on the down slope. Inevitably it was not long before he was a mere speck on the horizon, if visible at all. Although over the years neither of us readily conceded superiority to the other in any physical activity, here was one in which I resolved to compete no longer — he had demonstrated his supremacy on the *cordillera* and now had confirmed it. This was not easy for me to accept or to explain. Could it be that he was fitter and stronger than me? Definitely not! Could his short bandy legs be better suited to pedalling a bicycle than mine? Possibly. Could the gearing on his more expensive bike be more efficient than mine? Probably. There was no obvious explanation but I resolved to suppress my competitive instincts and proceed at my own pace. This meant that for the rest of the trip much of each day's cycling was a solitary experience, Roger a variable distance ahead, usually out of sight. At first I wished that he was less obsessed with speed and could resist the urge to pull away on the hills, but soon I realised that it is in solitude that one can best relate to one's surroundings. Who needs company when watching and listening to the sea crashing into a rocky shore, or when gazing out from a mountain-top across a broad panorama of rolling hills? The peace and tranquillity of solitude adds depth to such experiences. Alone on my bike, the only sound the quiet whine of tyres rolling over tarmac, I could commune privately with nature. Sometimes the solitude was temporarily broken on finding Roger resting by the roadside, waiting for me to catch up, but otherwise there was an understanding that our meeting place would be the *plaza mayor* in our previously-agreed destination, and I would arrive, exhausted, to find him in a café or bar, refreshed and relaxed, several beers ahead of me. I did point out to him that his wife would be furious if she knew he was breaking the agreement he had been forced to make with her. I remember, however, that she had predicted that he would not honour the agreement — she had always found it almost impossible to keep him within her sights.

A few miles north of Béjar there is a fairly long, demanding ascent, with snow-covered hills of the Sierra de Candelario to the south-east, but reaching the summit and passing the Puerto de Vallejero (3890ft) was rewarded with a long downhill ride into the town. On entering the town the road forks, with no indication of which leads to the town centre. I stopped and asked an elderly lady who was walking up the hill if she had seen a colourful cyclist pass by. She said she had not, but went on to welcome me to her town, telling me what a nice place it is and following up with details of her family history. She was certainly a friendly soul who I'm sure could have continued talking for much longer, but eventually I managed to break free, took the left fork as directed, which led to the Plaza de España where, sure enough, I found Roger comfortably settled at a café, nursing a few beers that he had thoughtfully (he said) set up to await my arrival.

We booked into the Hostal Residencia Blazquez Sanchez, just round the corner from the smart Hotel Colón. We had a quick look inside the hotel and noticed, more than anything else, the very attractive receptionist. Roger thought that he might talk her into offering us accommodation at a special reduced rate, but I convinced him that two sweaty and dishevelled cyclists would not be warmly welcomed in such a place and that even he, using his tried-and-tested charm technique, would be unlikely to impress the young lady. But he did succeed in persuading the *hostal* receptionist, a pleasant if rather less attractive young lady, to give him a double room for the price of a single — single rooms only had a shower, and he just had to have a bath, presumably in which to compose his next fax.

The Bar/Restaurante Metro was recommended to us. It was a large place, not one of the corridor-type bars so common in towns elsewhere. The spacious bar area was furnished with tables and chairs and at one end there was a large-screen TV, but what really caught the eye were the large photographs and posters of racing cyclists. We gathered that one of the town's most famous sons was a road racer called Lale Cubino. We were the only customers and the young barman was eager to articulate his few words of English. After a few *tapas* in the bar we were directed to the equally spacious adjoining restaurant where they insisted that we should order nothing but the very best — either they genuinely wanted to please us or they wanted to make up for their lack of customers that evening. A huge dish of their best (and expensive) *jamon iberico* and other cured pork delicacies was followed by enormous succulent steaks.

Back in the bar after our meal I asked where I could find a cycle shop in town, because I had not yet replaced the inner tube that I had used in place of the one punctured outside Toro. By chance, the owner of the local shop was now sitting at the bar with an attractive blonde, and he was proudly introduced to me as the brother of the great Lale Cubino. Unfortunately, he said, his shop was now closed and it would be closed next day because it was a day of *fiesta*. After a few moments' thought he asked me to wait and then left the bar. Twenty minutes later he was back. He had gone to his shop and brought me what I needed — and then stubbornly refused to accept payment for it. An impressive example of kindness and generosity, I thought, especially since it meant leaving his lovely friend with us — clearly he felt we were too old to pose a threat, which is a sad reflection of the truth.

We did not realise until the next day that we were not in the centre of the city. We had assumed that the Plaza de España, where we had met the previous day, was the *plaza mayor*, but in fact the old and more interesting part of the city is a short distance away to the west. Narrow streets suddenly open up into a spacious, quite impressive Plaza Mayor, with the 16th-century Palacio Ducal dominating at the top of a wide flight of steps and the 13th-century church of El Salvador in one corner. The town was the domain of a succession of dukes of Béjar until 1850, when Queen Isabel II declared it a city under the Crown; it now has a population of about 17,000.

CHAPTER 7
INTO EXTREMADURA
BÉJAR TO PLASENCIA

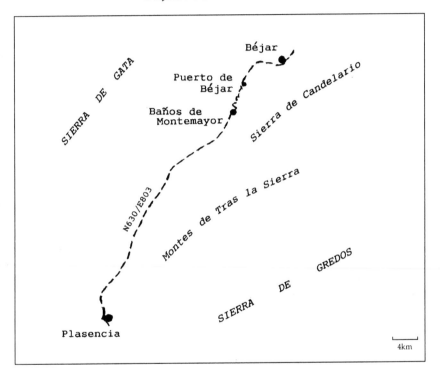

Béjar is at an altitude of about 3600ft and we had descended about 500ft to enter the town. On leaving we descended a little further, during which the impressive setting of the city could be admired high up on the right, before climbing again. About 10km south of Béjar we at last left Castilla y León, which had taken us four days to cross, entered Extremadura and began a long, zigzag descent of about 1000ft, flanked by hillsides yellow with gorse, into the town of Baños de Montemayor. We rode straight through the town, which is a spa holiday resort, and out into country where, for the first time, we saw dry-stone walls dividing the land into smaller fields, and cork oaks (*alcornoques*) as well as the ubiquitous holm oaks. The two types of oak are similar in appearance, but the leaves of the cork oak are a slightly lighter shade of green and, of course, many have their barks stripped off, an operation that is repeated every seven or eight years.

It was a perfect day, warm but with a light cooling breeze. I wore shorts for the first time — Roger had been displaying his bandy legs for a few days already. Not considering ourselves 'real' cyclists neither of us had bothered to kit ourselves with the colourful skin-tight outfits that proper cyclists wear. Other than a pair of lightweight Rohan trousers my clothing was ordinary everyday wear, while Roger, depending on the weather, looked (without his helmet) as if he was off to the golf course or to the beach.

The terrain was undulating again, but a long, fairly steep climb along the foothills of the Sierra de Gredos (the great range that extends to the north-east into central Spain) made me work hard before reaching Plasencia. We were, however, following the easiest route south, passing through a gap between the Sierra de Gredos and the Sierra de Gata to the west.

It was mid-afternoon before we reached Plasencia and we were famished. We had not passed through a town since Baños de Montemayor and therefore had eaten nothing since our breakfast *tostadas* in Béjar. Waving arms outside a bar caught my eye as I approached an aqueduct just outside the city walls — the urgent need for sustenance had driven Roger into the first bar he came across. The owner was a friendly middle-aged man notable especially for his size, or lack of it: he could not have been more than five feet tall and extremely thin. We asked for his biggest *plato combinado* and he did not disappoint us. As we were leaving he told us that his wife and three other ladies who were sitting with her at another table, having heard where we had come from and where we were going, were trying to guess our ages. None put us above 50.

Our morale and egos greatly boosted we rode down the hill, under the aqueduct, and down a narrow street into the Plaza Mayor, a rectangular *plaza* with a short avenue of trees down the middle, modest but pleasing buildings around it and arcades giving shelter to shops and cafés. Narrow cobbled streets without pavements radiate from all corners of the *plaza* but pedestrians are little disturbed by traffic because the main road runs outside the old city walls. We booked into the Hotel Rincon Extremeño, just off the Plaza Mayor. Here there was a problem finding a safe place to keep the bicycles, until a bright young man at the reception desk came up with the suggestion that we should put them in the manager's office. We wondered what the manager would have to say about this but we did as directed and hauled the bikes up a narrow staircase to his office. It was then explained that the manager was away for a couple of days. Our rooms were high up on the fourth floor, windows opening out on to the narrow street where children were playing, their loud shouts and laughter reverberating and gathering strength as they rose between the buildings. Children the world over shout and scream, but I wondered whether Spanish children do so even louder than others, as they learn to develop the power for which their seniors are famous. An afternoon nap here was out of the question.

Our wanderings in the evening took us to the cathedral at one end of the old city, just within the walls, and to the aqueduct at the other end, just outside the walls. The 12th-century walls are not easily seen from within the old city because houses have been built up against them, but they once incorporated more than 60 towers along their length which, together with the Rio Jerte that flows round three sides of the city, must have made the city almost impregnable. Outside the walls the city has expanded and now has a population of about 35,000.

The cathedral, which was closed, has an unusual shape, the result of an attempt to enlarge a small church by adding another back-to-back; when work on the second was abandoned in the middle of the 16th century it was simply blocked off. I found the aqueduct more interesting. A plaque on one of the arches indicates that it was built between 1566 and 1574. I counted nearly 50 arches, all of them intact, although some have been repaired and restored. It no longer serves a useful purpose but it is certainly an impressive structure. It runs part of its length over a beautifully kept public garden. Meeting a smartly dressed old gentleman I commented on how clean the garden was, and he replied that female gardeners take care of it — adding the very sexist comment that cleaning is what women do best. We walked with him to another attractive garden at the far end of the aqueduct, the Parque Los Pinos, where white peacocks and a variety of ducks, geese and other wildfowl screeched, quacked and squawked among pines and oaks.

Next morning, a bar open for *desayuno* (breakfast) offered *churros*, a popular Spanish breakfast food and a nice change from *tostadas*. *Churros* are made from a dough of flour and water which is squeezed out of a cylindrical container through a fine nozzle into a vat of hot oil. A length of dough is extruded in concentric circles and, by deft use of a wooden stick, flicked into the shape of a tight coil. After about one minute the *churros* are ready, and are cut up and eaten alone or with a little sugar, or dipped in coffee or hot chocolate. *Papas* are a popular alternative, made with potato flour in the same way, but they tend to be thinner and are turned out in small pear-shaped rings. *Churrerias*, small kiosks set up specifically to make *churros*, may be found in most Spanish towns, operating mainly at breakfast time, especially at weekends.

Aqueduct, Plasencia

CHAPTER 8
THE PARQUE NATURAL
DE MONTFRAGÜE
PLASENCIA TO TRUJILLO

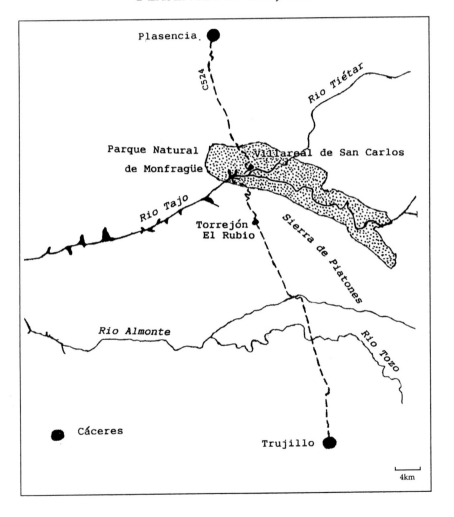

We left Plasencia for what was to be one of the highlights of the whole trip: the ride through the Parque Natural de Monfragüe and on to Trujillo. Maps warned us that there would be some hills to climb and even Roger (to my surprise) agreed that we were in no hurry and that we would walk up the steeper hills rather than exhaust ourselves. The first test came very soon after leaving Plasencia on the C524, and we both dismounted. We had walked barely 200 yards, however, when Roger was back on his bike, despite a long hill beckoning ahead. Challenged later on why he did not walk as previously agreed he explained that "walking feels like an unnatural activity". Although I could agree that our legs by that stage had become more attuned to cycling than to walking, his impatience to get back in the saddle also reflected his action-man nature: walking was just too slow and boring for him, unless it was to pursue a little white ball on a golf course. There was also something else driving him on: a computer. Attached to the handlebar of his bike, it recorded the distance covered each day, the highest speed reached during the day and, perhaps most important, the average speed, which certainly would have been adversely affected by walking. From this point on he was only forced off his bike, he told me, when he felt that the blood supply to his penis had been cut off and it was necessary to check that it was still there. I did not have this trouble (possible reasons for this cannot be discussed here) but I did have a recurring problem with the more posterior part of my anatomy, which most people rightly suppose must be a serious problem for any long-distance cyclist. Fortunately the problem was not soreness but numbness; soreness would have taken time to heal but numbness could be relieved by shifting weight off the saddle and on to the pedals on flat and, especially, on downhill sections. On long uphill sections, however, there was no way of relieving the discomfort except by dismounting. On one particularly long hill the discomfort built up to an intensity that convinced me that a bowel movement was imminent. I dismounted and started to look for a suitable spot off the road, only then realizing that the problem was simply an extremely numb backside.

On the first climb out of Plasencia, large tracts of Mediterranean lavender on the hillsides gave a foretaste of the delights that lay ahead. Soon the roadsides were embellished with tall bushes of white cistus and the yellows, pinks and purples of a wide variety of wild flowers, and off the road vast carpets of lavender covered the ground under the holm oaks. The road enters the Parque Natural de Monfragüe about 18km south of Plasencia through a rocky gorge lined with eucalyptus trees. The park is a fairly narrow tract of land about 35km long, extending only about 4km north and south of the great Rio Tajo (Tagus) that flows through it from east to west. The road twists and turns as it descends to the river and again as it ascends on the south side, crossing the river at a point just west of where it is joined by the Rio Tiétar. The scenery is spectacular. We stopped at Villareal de San Carlos, a hamlet north of the river that has one short street of stone cottages, a bar/restaurant, an information office and, at the lower end of the street, a small but interesting exhibition of the flora and fauna of the park. Established in 1979, the park is the only area in Extremadura that is protected from development and hunting. It provides sanctuary for a wide variety of wildlife, which is said to include the largest colony of black vultures in the world, the greatest concentrations of imperial eagles and of black storks, Griffon and Egyptian vultures, Peregrine falcons, golden eagles and eagle owls, as well as the rare Spanish lynx, red deer, wild boar, fox, wild cat and marten. A long list, and no doubt many others could be added. On the move on a bicycle it would have been a stroke of luck to see any of the rarer species, but even with my limited powers of observation (which Roger reckoned are incapable of identifying a crow at more than ten paces — a slight exaggeration) I spotted several vultures and an eagle. It was impossible, however, not to see and be dazzled by the profusion of wild flowers. We were travelling at the time of year when wild flowers are at their best in that region, and they added an extra dimension to the outstanding natural beauty of the landscape.

Having worked hard climbing out of the park after crossing the river, I was in dire need of refreshment and sustenance. Roger had gone on ahead and I was delighted when I saw him sitting outside one of the two bar/restaurants facing one another at Torrejón el Rubio, the only place between Plasencia and

Rio Tajo, Parque Natural de Monfragüe

Trujillo, other than Villareal, where such facilities are available. The road continues on an undulating course through grasslands covered with the ubiquitous holm oak, much of it fenced off and maintained as private hunting reserves. The road descends to cross the Rio Almonte, climbs again, descends again to cross the Rio Tozo and then climbs again; hard work for a cyclist but rewarded by the wonderful scenery, with the rocky crags of the Sierra de Platones forming an impressive backdrop to the east.

Quite suddenly, about 15km from Trujillo, the wooded hunting reserves give way to an almost tree-less, rocky landscape, stone walls enclosing fields strewn with granite boulders. Lying against one of these, by a deserted shepherd's hut, I found Roger, who had quickly disappeared into the distance soon after we had left Torrejón el Rubio. In the next field was a herd of huge black bulls, of the type bred for the bullring, looking docile as they grazed peacefully in the sunshine, blissfully unaware that one day they would hold centre stage before a roaring crowd in some hot and dusty *plaza de toros* before suffering humiliation and a bloody death.

Bridge over Rio Almonte

65

Trujillo was already in sight in the distance and, as we got closer, the walls of the town and castle impressively dominated the skyline. Narrow streets inevitably led to the Plaza Mayor, unusual in being triangular. From a café at the base (eastern side) of the triangle the eye is first drawn to the centre, to the large bronze equestrian statue of Trujillo's most famous son, Francisco Pizarro, the conqueror of Peru. Left of the apex of the triangle is the Palacio de la Conquista, one of the Pizarro family mansions, and down in the right-hand corner, up a broad flight of steps, the rather austere church of San Martín, crowned with storks' nests. It is an interesting *plaza* despite some of the central area being used as a car park. Above, there was a dazzling display of bird-life, hundreds of martins and swifts screaming, wheeling and darting in frantic activity and, hovering high above them, more than one kind of bird of prey (which even Roger was unable to identify).

After absorbing the scene over several glasses of cool beer I set out to find an *hostal* or *pensión* (I still do not understand the distinction between the two — perhaps there is none). Opposite the church of San Martín, at the entrance of the grand Palacio de los Duques de San Carlos (now a nuns' residence) I was approached politely by a lady in a furry brown coat and asked if I was looking for accommodation. She just happened to be the owner of the Pensión Boni a few yards down the narrow street and had obviously been hovering at the street corner ready to grab a likely customer, rather like one of those Alaskan grissly brown bears that stand over fast-moving rapids ready to pounce on a juicy pink salmon.

The *pensión* was an attractive old house with marble floors and tiled walls, and spotlessly clean (as were all the other *hostales* and *pensiónes* we had encountered). Roger took the most expensive room, a double room looking out over a small internal *patio*, and I took a cheap single room facing the street. This was a mistake, something to be avoided in old Spanish towns, especially when it is hot and windows are kept open, because those infernal two-stroke machines so popular in Spain can make one's life a misery. Here, turning into the narrow street at the Palacio, their spluttering drone increased in a crescendo and exploded under

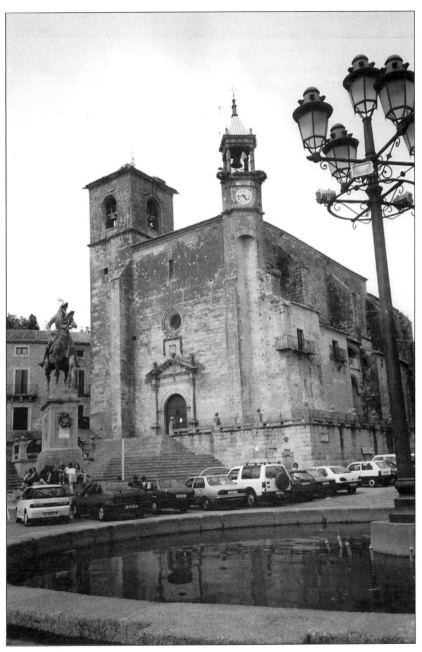

Church of San Martín, and Pizarro statue, Trujillo

67

my window. While Roger luxuriated in his all-mod-cons room, I felt I was being constantly attacked by angry hornets.

After a few drinks and *tapas* around the Plaza Mayor we strolled up to the old town on the hill. Enclosed by old Moorish walls are several interesting buildings associated with, among others, the Pizarro and Orellana families (Francisco Orellana, another famous son of Trujillo, was the first explorer of the Amazon), and the church of Santa Maria Mayor where members of the Pizarro family are entombed. Francisco Pizarro was born in 1475, the illegitimate son of a poor Trujillo family; he had three brothers, two of whom were also illegitimate. The discovery of the New World by Columbus in October 1492 had opened up opportunites for adventure and a new life for men like the Pizarros. Furthermore, the long-running battles with the Moors had finally ended in January 1492 with the fall of Granada, and many men of the Christian armies found themselves unemployed. It is not difficult to imagine that many, especially those from relatively poor lands like Extremadura, must have been attracted by the prospect of riches in the New World. Hernán Cortés was one of them. Born in 1485 in the Extremaduran town of Medellín, about 70km south of Trujillo, he conquered Mexico in 1521, defeating the Aztecs with, it is claimed, only about 600 men. Amazingly, Francisco Pizarro and his brothers are said to have defeated the Incas in Peru with even fewer men. Spanish weapons and military techniques were, no doubt, superior, but another important factor was the devastating effect that smallpox and other European diseases had already had on the native populations. Pizarro established the city and capital of Peru, Lima, in which there is an statue of him identical to the one in Trujillo.

At the north end of the town stand the remains of the castle, with impressive, well-restored walls around which swooped large numbers of grey-naped jackdaws. From the ramparts there is a superb view over the town and east to the distant hills of the Sierra de Guadalupe. The town stands at an altitude of 1591ft and has a population of about 10,000.

Still hungry, we decided to try the Meson La Troya on the Plaza Mayor, which opened early (8pm, early for Spain). A rather

Trujillo — castle and view of Plaza Mayor from ramparts

gruff waiter ushered us to a table and no sooner had we sat down that he planted huge plates of potato omelette and salad, and a bottle of red wine, on the table. When I suggested that it might be a good idea if he showed us a menu he simply rattled off at high speed all the alternatives on offer, taking no account of the possibility that we might not be fluent in Spanish. He did not take kindly to my request to repeat it all, slowly. The main courses were even larger than the starter, and by the end the meal was voted one the biggest we had ever eaten but the worst presented. We left no tip.

It had been a great day. The 80km ride from Plasencia had been hard at times but always a delight. Not only was the scenery spectacular, especially within the park, but there was hardly any traffic, because the main road between Plasencia and Trujillo takes a different route, passing through Cáceres.

CHAPTER 9
EMERITA AUGUSTA
TRUJILLO TO MÉRIDA

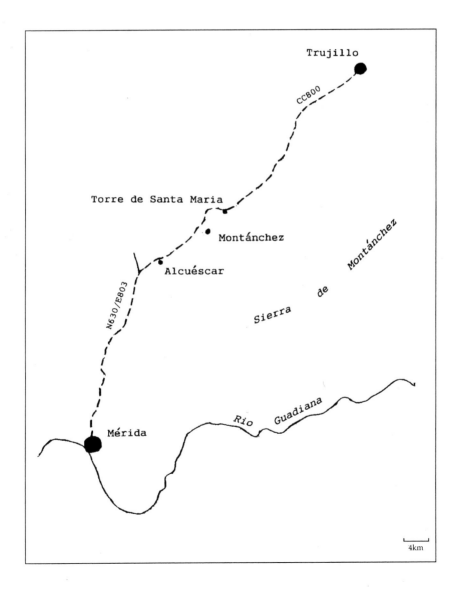

We next headed for Mérida along another almost traffic-free minor road (CC800), first across rocky, bare terrain similar to that just north of Trujillo, and then across pleasant undulating grasslands, with cattle, pigs and sheep grazing amongst the holm oaks, and the hills of the Sierra de Montánchez on our left. Around here olive groves made their first appearance, and the blue-purple carpets under the trees were of bristly bugloss instead of lavender, but equally spectacular. There were only a few isolated villages on the 80km stretch to Mérida. We stopped for a drink in a bar opposite the church in Torre de Santa Maria, where two surly men in the bar and a sad donkey in the street were the only signs of life. On the road again we passed Montánchez, high up on the hill above the road. The town is an important centre for the production of *jamon ibérico*, the cured ham that is made from the black pigs (related to wild boar) that roam freely throughout Extremadura feeding on holm oak acorns. This is the type of ham that Spaniards recognize as real ham. They call our type *jamon york* and consider it very inferior — it is unlikely to be found in any self-respecting bar in Extremadura. Several large hams hang behind every bar, and they get through them at a surprising rate considering how thinly it is always cut and how expensive it is.

By the time we reached the turning to Alcuéscar our stomachs were crying out for food, so we were more than pleased to find the aptly-named Bar Oasis at the roadside, where we gorged on a huge *cocido de cerdo* (pork stew).

The CC801 must be well off the beaten path for all except the small local population, yet our appearance in the Bar Oasis, as in the bar at Torre de Santa Maria, generated surprisingly little interest. Our greeting of *"buenos dias"* was politely acknowledged but we could get little more out of them. The children outside showed greater interest, especially in our *bicis* (bikes). This apparent lack of interest in a couple of obvious foreigners was an attitude which, unfortunately, we encountered frequently on our journey. Nowhere did we find the people unpleasant but often they were disappointingly cold and uninterested. A welcome exception was a lonely old shepherd we stopped to talk to near Torre de Santa Maria. Perhaps because of the loneliness of his job

Roger with shepherd

he was eager to tell us about himself and his life, and was interested to hear what we were doing. Several generations of his family had eeked out a modest but happy living from the land, but now, he said sadly, the young desert the country in search of a faster, more exciting life in the cities — a familiar story. Shepherds are seldom seen in Britain nowadays but they are a frequent sight in Extremadura; although there are some enclosed fields, sheep more commonly roam open grassland, supervised all day by a shepherd who ensures they keep together and off the road. As we left we said *"adios"* and he said *"hasta luego"*. We had heard this expression before and were to hear it many times again; literally it means 'see you later' or 'until the next time'. Spaniards often seem to prefer to use these parting words even with strangers whom they are unlikely to meet again — and it could safely be predicted that we would not meet this shepherd again.

Soon after leaving the Bar Oasis, heavily laden with *cocido*, we joined the main road (N630/E803) on which we had travelled from Salamanca to Plasencia. Suddenly, about 6km north of Mérida, the landscape changed, the grasslands and holm oaks that had dominated for several days giving way to large fields of cereal crops and some vines. I entered Mérida by crossing a 4-arch Roman bridge over the Rio Albarregas (a tributary of the Guadiana) and riding parallel to a half-mile-long Roman aqueduct, the Acueducto de los Milagros, which is over 80ft high and has most of its arches intact. Roger got there well before me and I found him in the Plaza de España, Mérida's *plaza mayor*, a pleasant, restful, place with cafés at each corner. The *plaza* is shaded by tall palm trees and clipped orange trees, a change from the pollarded plane trees that were such a consistent feature in Castilla y León. The buildings around the *plaza* are attractive if unremarkable, the most impressive being the Hotel Emperatrix. Typically, Roger wanted to head straight for the hotel, but I just managed to hold him back and persuade him that we should seek more modest accommodation, which seems, to me at least, more appropriate for bikers than first-class hotels. With some difficulty I gained the attention of a group of middle-aged ladies who were sitting around a nearby table talking excitedly and

Roman aqueduct, Mérida

incessantly (as only ladies can do) and asked if they could recommend an *hostal*. Predictably each came up with a different suggestion, all at the same time, so it was in a confused state that we left them, passed under a Roman arch (the Arco de Trajano), which was the north gate of the Roman city, and up to the *parador* on the Plaza de la Constitución. There are currently 85 *paradores* in Spain, all first-class, State-run hotels, many of them especially interesting for having been built within an old castle, monastery or other historic building. This one in Mérida has an interesting and varied history, having served as a convent, a hospital, a mental asylum and even as a prison — it was converted to a *parador* in 1933. As I struggled again to restrain Roger I noticed a sign 'Hostal Senero' on a wall at a corner of the *plaza*. We found the *hostal* just a hundred yards down the Calle Holguín, an old house, squeaky clean, with typical tiled walls and marble floors and a small internal *patio*. For 2400 pesetas (about £10) we each had a small but comfortable room with *en suite* bathroom, considerably better value than the rate Roger might have negotiated in the hotel or *parador*. I had a long soak in the bath, and a nap disturbed only by the clatter of storks on the rooftops, which was much less disruptive than the children in Plasencia or the mopeds in Trujillo.

Later, we set out to explore the local bars. There was no shortage of them in the narrow streets around the Plaza de España. Most of them were of the bare, long-corridor type, but more interesting was the Bar Benito in the Calle San Francisco, its walls from floor to ceiling smothered with photographs and posters of bullfighters and bullfights. One of the posters particularly caught my eye: the one advertising the *corrida* in Linares on the 28th of August 1947 in which the great matador Manolete was fatally injured. The *raciónes* were good too: *sardinas asadas* (grilled sardines), *torta de espinaca* (spinach pie) and *riñones al Jerez* (kidneys in sherry sauce).

We were ahead of schedule. We had estimated that we would take about 3 weeks to reach Gibraltar from Santander and my wife was flying out to meet us on arrival. We were now only on our tenth day and therefore we decided to take a rest by remaining in Mérida the next day. After all, Mérida was once, as Emerita Augusta, the capital of the Roman province of Lusitania and now contains more Roman remains than any other Spanish city. Mérida was one of the important cities along a Roman road now referred to as the Via de la Plata that linked the south-western port of Ayamonte with the northern port of Gijon, via Béjar, Salamanca and Astorga. The population in Roman times was about 50,000, the largest Roman city in Iberia; now it is only about 40,000. The Via de la Plata was also used by pilgrims travelling to Santiago de Compostela from the south of the country.

We spent the morning at the most important Roman site, where a theatre and an amphitheatre stand side by side. The theatre, which was completed in about 15-16BC, has a large, banked semi-circular seating area that can accommodate 6000 people, and a magnificent stage backed by a row of 24 tall columns (if I counted correctly) supporting, above them, a second row of slightly shorter columns. Behind the stage is a garden surrounded by yet more columns. The much simpler oval-shaped amphitheatre was planned at the same time as the theatre but not completed until some years later, in 8BC. It could

Roman theatre, Mérida

accommodate 15,000 spectators at gladiatorial contests, fights between wild animals and, most popular, fights between men and wild animals. The theatre and amphitheatre, such busy centres of activity during Roman times, fell into disuse and were largely abandoned during the centuries that followed. Excavation and restoration of the sites, which began in 1910, have brought them back to life, especially the theatre which has, since 1933, been the venue each year for a festival of classical plays. Just outside the city is the Circo Romano, which was built in about 1BC; it could accommodate as many as 30,000 people, and staged chariot races and other sporting spectacles in an oval arena over $1/4$ mile long and over 100 yards long, but we did not visit it mainly because we were told that little of it remains — but also, it must be admitted, because we were too lazy to walk there.

After lunch we strolled along the half-mile-long, 60-arch Roman bridge across the Rio Guadiana, the third of the four great rivers that flow west into the Atlantic (we had already crossed the Duero in Toro and the Tajo in the Parque Natural de Monfragüe). The bridge is one of the longest Roman bridges remaining in the world; it is now for pedestrians only but until the elegant Puente de Lusitania was completed a few hundred yards up river in December 1993 it was the main thoroughfare across the river. Ramps from the bridge run down to a mid-river island, from which there is an excellent view of the imposing walls of the *alcazaba*, the Moorish fortress built on the site of a Roman fortification defending the bridge.

We could not get inside the *alcazaba* because it was closed. A problem for tourists in Spain is that life almost comes to a stand-still at about 1 or 2 o'clock in the afternoon. Shops, banks, offices, many tourist sites and even tourist information offices, all close, the workers go home, eat a substantial lunch, then fall asleep, and the town does not come alive again until about 5pm. (There must, however, be an increasing number of Spaniards who have been forced, as employees of multi-national companies that have flooded into Spain during the last 20 years, to adopt a *siesta*-less lifestyle.) Although the afternoon shutdown can be very frustrating for foreign tourists, the Spanish system does have its com-

Roman bridge and Moorish alcazaba, Mérida

pensations because, sustained by a good lunch and rested after their *siesta*, Spaniards do not immediately rush home when they finish work at about 8pm but instead sit and chat in cafés and bars or just walk about town, especially around their *plaza mayor*, participating in the traditional Spanish *paseo*. Evenings in even the most modest Spanish towns are therefore full of life whereas in many comparable towns in Britain, for example, they are dead. Young couples, children of all ages, senior citizens, all mingle happily in the cool of the evening. The atmosphere is friendly and relaxed, and nowhere did we see any of the loutish behaviour from youngsters that we sometimes have to tolerate in our towns. No doubt the Spanish summer climate has greatly influenced their lifestyle, the heat of the afternoon forcing them indoors and the cool of the evening bringing them out. Another factor encouraging the Spanish *paseo* must be the fact that most Spaniards live in apartments close to their city centres, not in houses with gardens in the suburbs. While on hot summer evenings the British stay at home and enjoy (or work in) their gardens, Spaniards leave their apartments and join the *paseo*. We were pleased to enjoy their lively evenings, and were only rarely inconvenienced by their moribund afternoons because we were usually slogging it out on the roads at that time.

After failing to gain entry to the *alcazaba*, I decided I would follow the Spaniards' example and return to our *hostal* for a *siesta* (I had some sleep to catch up on after my disturbed night in Trujillo). Roger carried on and visited the very interesting Museo Nacional de Arte Romano, a large, purpose-built, modern brick building completed in 1985 close to the theatre/amphitheatre complex. Most impressive among the wide range of exhibits, I was told, were huge wall-mounted mosaics that can be viewed from any of the three levels of the open-plan interior. Later we had an 'up market' dinner in the grand dining room of the Hotel Emperatriz, a rare treat which Roger persuaded me we deserved at this stage of our journey. There we observed, not for the first time, a polite Spanish custom: people making their way to a table in a restaurant acknowledging those already dining nearby with the words *"que aproveche"*, which loosely translated means "enjoy your meal", the equivalent of the French *"bon apetit"*. We British, of course, walk by minding our own business.

Having breakfast next morning in a café on the Plaza de España, I watched storks preening themselves on a huge nest on top of the church of Santa Maria la Mayor across the *plaza*. The nest, like many others we had seen, was sitting so precariously on the edge of a narrow ledge that it was amazing it stayed up there. I asked a man at the next table whether the storks or their nests ever cause any problems. The main danger, I was told, is that a nest occasionally comes crashing down and damages a building or injures a passer-by. Despite this danger, Spaniards consider storks to be harbingers of good fortune and that it is a privilege to have them nest on their rooftop. To minimize the risk, bowl-shaped wire frameworks are firmly secured to the top of many churches and tall buildings in the hope that storks will build their nests within them. Storks seem to like them — we never saw one unoccupied.

CHAPTER 10
TOWARDS ANDALUCÍA
MÉRIDA TO LLERENA

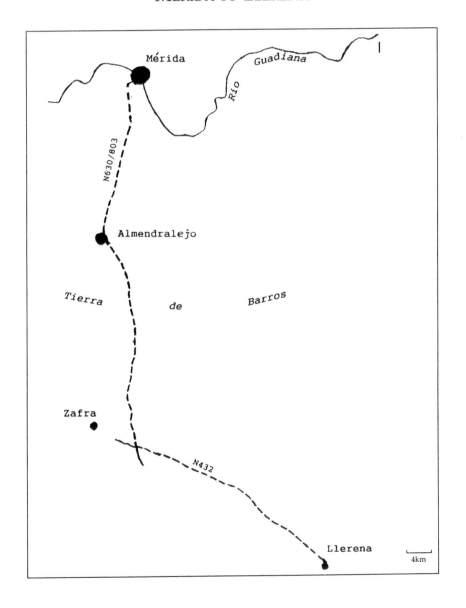

We left Mérida by crossing the Guadiana on the new Puente de Lusitania, and continued south on the N630/E803. The terrain was the flattest we had encountered since north of Salamanca, and this, as well as the smooth road surface, enabled us to make good progress. The land was heavily cultivated with cereal crops, as it had been for a few miles north of Mérida. Then, rather abruptly, vineyards appeared, covering vast areas across the red earth of the Tierra de Barros, and olive trees began to out-number holm oaks. After a short break for a drink in a small roadside hotel on the southern outskirt of Almendralejo, we sped down towards Zafra. We had planned to visit Zafra, which is well known principally for its great castle, now a *parador*, but the momentum we had gathered carried us on. A bar/restaurant at the intersection with the N432, the only watering hole on the road since Almendralejo, was perfectly placed for our lunch stop, after which we headed east along the N432 to Llerena. (The main route south continues on the N630/E803 to Sevilla, but we decided to avoid the big city and the heavy traffic that would inevitably be associated with it.) A café in the Plaza Mayor in Llerena, opposite the imposing white church of La Virgen de la Granada with its tall stone tower, was a welcome resting place after what had been our longest ride so far: 101km. The church is rather unusual, all white except for its stone tower, looking a bit like a wedding cake with a chocolate wafer stuck in it. It has gal-leries on two levels facing the *plaza*, each having 18 arches and wrought-iron railings. Above, on the edge of the orange tiled roof, stands a balustrade topped with ornamental arrow-shaped pinnacles, a feature that is continued on other buildings around the *plaza*. A group of young teenagers was playing in the *plaza* and soon our relaxation was rudely disturbed as our presence attracted their attention. I suppose nothing much changes from day to day in a small town like Llerena, so it was not unreason-able that the arrival of strangers should have stimulated their interest (though, as we had previously noted, not of their elders). Approaching furtively at first they opened with "You English?", then "Good afternoon", moving on to "What's your name?", "How old are you?". They told us they were learning English at school and obviously they were keen to practise, the boys quite

*Vineyard, Tierra de
Barros*

*Church of La Virgen
de la Granada,
Llerena*

83

boldly, the girls rather shyly. As they gained confidence they came closer, eventually swarming all over us and becoming increasingly noisy and cheeky. It was all good fun but it was clearly necessary to control the situation before it got completely out of hand. With some difficulty I managed to persuade them to return to their games in the *plaza*. We left soon after to shouts of "Goodbye, goodbye". The one *hostal* in the town, the Hostal los Angeles, seemed so drab that we went back to one we had passed on the road just outside the town, the Hostal Gallego. The owner was another of the surly, unwelcoming type, but offered comfortable rooms at the ridiculous price of 1000 pesetas (just over £4) for me and a little more for a room with *en suite* facilities for my more demanding companion. An equally surly waiter served us an excellent meal after which there was nothing to do but to turn in early.

The *hostal* is set back a little from the road but, nevertheless, heavy lorries thundering past throughout the night disturbed my sleep. Once again I had made the mistake of taking a room facing a road — will I ever learn? Next morning I was awakened by a large bus drawing up outside my window and disgorging a load of chattering children, who had a drink, used the toilet and then, mercifully, were taken away.

CHAPTER 11
THE SIERRA MORENA
LLERENA TO CONSTANTINA

On the next leg of our journey we would leave Extremadura, through which we had cycled for four days, and enter Andalucía. I had expected Extremadura to be barren, dusty and desert-like, based on Robin Neilland's account of his walk from Santander to Gibraltar in which he describes Extremadura as "a real desert in the middle of Spain" and "quite remarkably bleak". Instead, my lasting impression is of rolling grasslands dotted with holm oaks, spectacular landscapes of hills, rivers and wild flowers, fertile agricultural land, vineyards and olive groves. Only in the area around Trujillo could the land reasonably be described as desert-like. It is possible that Neilland's route, although only 50-80km east of ours, crosses more barren country, or, because his walk was in October, the land had been scorched by the summer sun.

The day ahead was to rival for enjoyment the one from Plasencia to Trujillo. Our target for the day was Constantina, only 65km away, but the Sierra Morena was ahead of us; it looked fearsome on my map, and I was expecting to be severely tested and to have to do some walking. However, it was easy going for the first 15km or so, riding on a ridge in the foothills of the *sierra* with magnificent views across a flat plain to the east, after which it became a little more testing as the road threaded its way through rolling hills covered with olive trees, their attractive silver-grey foliage shimmering in the breeze and their dark, irregular trunks in sharp relief against the pink earth.

There is a sharp descent into Guadalcanal. Coming down the hill, the town lies spread out on the right, a ribbon of squat white buildings with orange tiled roofs, the church at the far end, dominant as ever. We had a quick look at the town, riding as far as the church and back again, along narrow streets between dazzling whitewashed houses, and then stopped at the Bar Andrea on the way out of town. So far, surprisingly, there had been no really steep hills. I asked a *guardia civil* in the bar where the hills start but, again to my surprise, he said there were none. I didn't know whether to believe him, but the next section again was no more demanding than what we had already negotiated. We stopped for lunch in a bar at the southern end of the small town of San Nicolas del Puerto where a friendly man-and-wife team served up a satisfying *plato combinado*. They told us we must see the source of a river just off the road a hundred yards or so from their bar, which we duly did — a bubbling pool in a peaceful spot, shaded by trees, just the place, I thought, to lie down and have a *siesta*, a temptation that was resisted with some difficulty.

We were now within another *parque natural*, which stretches over a huge area across the Sierra Morena and in this region is known as the Parque Natural de Sevilla. As in the Parque Natural de Monfragüe the roadsides were ablaze with the colours of wild flowers: white and pink cistus, blue-purple bristly bugloss, yellow broom, gorse, red poppy and many more. Strangely, olive trees, so prevalent north of Guadalcanal, were now absent, the holm oak again predominating across the undulating grassland. The *guardia civil* was right: there were no big hills. The reason began to sink in: we had entered the Sierra Morena from the Extremaduran *meseta*, much of which is at an altitude of 1500-2000ft, so we had not climbed much because the average altitude of the *sierra* is only about 2000ft. (It would have been quite different if we had entered the *sierra* from the south, as we would see the following day.)

I arrived in Constantina in mid-afternoon, some time after Roger. Finding the *plaza mayor* presented a problem because the town, unusually, does not have one. I was directed to a short pedestrianized street, the Calle Mesones, which is the closest they have to a *plaza mayor*, and walked up and down looking for Roger in the various bars, without success. I sat at a table outside an *heladeria* (ice cream parlour). Being mid-afternoon, the town was becalmed — two old men sitting opposite, outside the Bar El Moderno, the only sign of life on the Calle Mesones. As I sucked contentedly at my ice cream I reflected on what a wonderful day it had been: sunshine, almost no traffic, rolling hills dotted with oak and olive trees, the profusion of wild flowers — simply idyllic.

Stirring myself, I walked round a corner beyond the pedestrianized section and there was Roger in a bar, the Bodeguita Tomas, only about 50 yards from where I had been sitting. The men there were in high spirits, apparently having preferred a few drinks to a *siesta*. I asked them about the two *fondas* men-

Sierra Morena

tioned in *The Rough Guide,* and was told that they had both closed. They suggested, instead, a *casa de huespedes* (guest house) owned by a lady called Maripepa. Mention of her name generated several minutes of noisy banter between them, from which we gathered that she was an attractive lady after whom at least one of them had lusted in the past — with what success we were not able to judge. We set out eagerly to meet the lady. Her house, in the Calle José de la Bastida, stood out from the others in the whitewashed row because of its mature brick facade and the decorative lintels over its doors and windows. The lady who opened the door was obviously Maripepa, an elegant, well-dressed lady, now middle-aged but clearly one who in her youth must have excited the young lads of the town, including the rabble in the bar from whom she was quick to dissociate herself when we told her who had sent us. An arched doorway with an fine wrought-iron gate led to an extremely attractive internal *patio*, its walls to shoulder level adorned with beautiful tiles and above with pictures and decorative plates. A wide marble staircase with wrought-iron balustrade led from the *patio* to first-floor rooms beautifully furnished with solid, old, dark-wood furniture, with full-length windows and wrought-iron balconies opening out over the *patio.* The house had recently been redecorated and several improvements made, and I suspect that she has plans to reap a higher reward for her efforts than the 2500 pesetas (just over £10) she charged us which, unusually for Spain, included breakfast.

We emerged later from her house into a scene transformed from the almost deserted, sleepy place we had found on arrival. Now it was bustling with people enjoying their *paseo*, walking up and down the Calle Mesones socializing with fellow towns-folk, the young parading as if on a catwalk for inspection by the opposite sex. Not so many years ago, before Spanish youth took advantage of post-Franco freedom to embrace the permissive lifestyles popularized in North America and Britain, the *paseo* was invariably the preliminary stage in the courting process. Boys and girls would eye each other cautiously for several weeks as their paths crossed before exchanging furtive smiles, and several more weeks might pass before they made verbal contact and began walking together, followed by another interval before making physical contact by holding hands. Nowadays this traditional ritual is greatly foreshortened (except, perhaps, in isolated rural communities): progress is often faster to the bedroom now than it was to the exchange of smiles in the past.

Constantina is a pleasant little city with a population of about 10,000; it was granted city status by Alfonso XIII in 1916. It is strung out in a narrow strip between the hills, its castle, the Castillo de la Armada, high above it. While Roger sorted out his faxes and postcards, I walked up the steep hillside, zigzagging along a maze of narrow lanes between fascinating old houses, to the castle, from which there is a bird's eye view of the whole city and valley. The castle was captured from the Moors by Fernando III in 1247; only a section of the walls and three of its original seven towers remain.

Maripepa had recommended a bar/restaurant, the Cambio Tercio, owned by her son. It is at the top end of the city, past a wide *alameda* shaded by tall trees and flanked by market stalls. The decor of the Cambio Tercio suggests that the son has inherited some sense of style from his mother. The furnishings are pleasantly rustic and the walls are covered with old photographs of local scenes, and portraits and action photographs of famous bullfighters. After a few tasty *tapas* we enjoyed superb *raciónes* of *tortilla de espárrago* (asparagus omelette) and *cocido de venado* (venison stew) in the bar; the restaurant was not open yet — at 8.30pm it was too early for locals to think about dinner. Sitting at a table near the bar I noticed something quite extraordinary: several small plastic litter bins attached to the customers' side of the bar. Was Maripepa's son really suggesting that his customers should dispose of their litter in these bins, against the long-standing and accepted practice of throwing it all on the floor ? We did not stay long enough to assess whether, over the course of an evening, it was the bins or the floor that collected the most litter.

CHAPTER 12
DESCENT INTO THE GUADALQUIVIR VALLEY

Constantina to Carmona

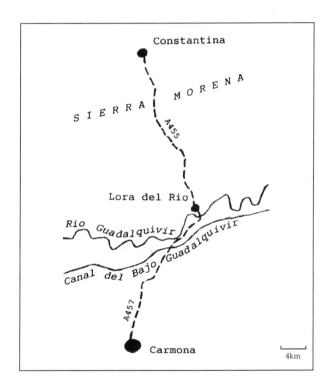

Next morning Maripepa gave us breakfast in her pleasant kitchen, keeping up a constant stream of chatter while preparing our *tostadas*, during which we were able to examine her more closely than was possible on our brief meeting the previous evening. Her facial features are classical Andalucian Gypsy, with dark, lively eyes, olive-brown skin, and jet-black hair swept tightly back and held in a bun. She is a vivacious widow with five grown-up children (two of whom visited her while we were having breakfast), and she enjoys a lively social life, proudly boasting of friendship with Litri, the famous bullfighter. She introduced us to a different kind of *tostada*; instead of spreading the bread with butter she spiked it heavily with a knife, then poured olive oil with garlic into it and gave it a final gentle toasting under the grill. It certainly made a tasty alternative to the normal butter-and-jam *tostada*.

I was still apprehensive about the *sierra*, finding it difficult to believe that we could have such an easy ride across it, but we were again reassured that the road did not climb significantly on its course south and, indeed, that after about 20km it would be all downhill. So we set out for Carmona expecting an easy day's ride because after descending from the *sierra* we would be on the flat plain of south-west Spain. But it was not to be!

The day started well enough, among the oaks, olive groves and wild flowers of the *sierra* — carpets of blue-purple bugloss being particularly spectacular — followed by a long descent to Lora del Rio that opened up great vistas to the south. At last, sadly, we were leaving the *meseta*, on which we had travelled since crossing the Cantabrian mountains, descending from about 2000ft to less than 300ft in the Guadalquivir valley. Past Lora we soon crossed the Rio Guadalquivir, the last of the four great Spanish rivers flowing into the Atlantic that we had crossed on our journey. The Guadalquivir runs for 815km from the Sierra de Cazorla, north-east of Granada, but for the last 650km it drops only about 1000ft through an increasingly flat valley that widens as the river flows slowly westwards past Córdoba and Sevilla, providing a vast expanse of fertile agricultural land that is intensively cultivated with cereal and vegetable crops.

The problems of the day began soon after crossing the river:

major road works lay ahead. It was only about 20km to Carmona but that short distance was to present a stern test. The road surface was appalling all the way, loose stones making progress on a bicycle slow and a little hazardous. I had expected the terrain between Lora and Carmona to be dead flat but it was not, and, unable to get up any speed on the rough road surface, even small inclines were quite demanding. Another factor contributing to my discomfort was the heat. It was by far the hottest day we had experienced on our trip, partly due, no doubt, to the fact that we were no longer benefiting from the altitude of the *meseta*. The landscape, also, had changed dramatically. Gone were the trees and grasslands of the *sierra*; here every inch of land was cultivated, vast fields extending as far as the eye could see, and not a tree in sight. To put it mildly, it was no fun, in complete contrast to the sheer delight recently experienced in the Sierra Morena. Eventually a row of trees extending to the roadside beckoned like an oasis in a desert, so inviting that I was surprised not to find Roger sheltering there. I sat under the nearest tree, ate a *bocadillo* I had bought in Lora, drank warm water from my on-bike bottle and tried hard to summon the will-power to continue. It was then that I decided that the comfort of a stay at the famous *parador* in Carmona would go some way to compensate for the hardships of the afternoon. For the rest of the way this was the 'carrot' that I kept firmly in mind. As I ground my way slowly towards my goal, now visible on a hill in the distance, I retained a mental picture of myself jumping into the *parador*'s pool and then reclining on a poolside sunbed, with a drink at hand. I could not wait to get there but somehow the place on the hill took a long time to come closer. At last a final short effort took me into the town and all I had to do was find the *parador*. I entered the *ciudad vieja* (old city) through the Roman Puerta de Sevilla, then worked my way up narrow cobbled streets following the *'parador'* signs, my impatience to jump into the pool building up to a climax. Eventually I got there — and was dealt a shattering blow. A large sign in several languages announced that the *parador* was closed for major repairs. I cannot describe my feelings at that moment. I was exhausted, drenched in sweat, and what had sustained me for the last hour or so had proved to

Moorish gateway in the Puerta de Sevilla, Carmona

be unattainable. I slumped over my bicycle and was prepared to die, but just in time I remembered how a few beers can lift one's spirits, so I set off to find the *plaza mayor*, which in Carmona is called the Plaza de San Fernando.

I rode round the circular *plaza* and there, at a café, I spotted Roger's waving arms — the team captain flagging in his straggler. Too impatient to wait for the services of a waiter, I stormed into the bar and demanded a huge glass of beer, indicating with two hands the size of glass I had in mind. Beer in Spain is normally dispensed in a glass holding barely half a pint, which was no good to me at that time. To my surprise he produced an authentic British dimpled pint mug with handle, which I had not seen in Spain before or seen since, calling it a *jarro* (a jug), and I ordered two of them for starters, the first hardly touching the sides of my gullet. It had been a hard day.

An obliging waiter did us the favour of telephoning a nearby *pensión* to check room availability. Bookings confirmed, we made our way down to the Pensión Comercio, which is built against the Moorish city wall just inside the Puerta de Sevilla. More modest than Maripepa's excellent establisment in Constantina it was, nevertheless, perfectly satisfactory: an attractive internal *patio* and rooms on the first floor opening over it. Collapsing on to the bed I instantly sank into a deep trance. Unfortunately, intruding into this blissful state was the voice of Antonio, the owner, in full flow in the *patio* below, his voice reverberating around the *patio* and up through the house. It was a veritable *tour de force* lasting nearly two hours, all the more amazing because there seemed to be no responding voice. It was a virtuoso solo performance, of the sort (dare I say) normally associated with a woman. In my trance-like state it was a minor irritation; if I had been awake it would have been intolerable. Internal *patios* are designed to be quiet and peaceful refuges from the outside world but they are not when people like Antonio are around.

Eventually restored to full consciousness I met Roger again in the Plaza de San Fernando, joining the local folk in their evening *paseo*. The *plaza* is surrounded by pleasant if unspectacular buildings, the grandest being the city hall (Carmona was granted city status by Felipe IV in 1630) and the adjoining church of San

Salvador. I was surprised not to see a stork's nest on the church or, indeed, on any of the other buildings around the *plaza*; on reflection, I realised I had not seen one since we left Mérida. Why are they so prevalent in Castilla y León and Extremadura and absent (or much less prevalent) further south? No doubt several factors are involved, including climate and the availability of their sources of food (fish, frogs, small reptiles and insects), but it is surprising that there are so many in the agricultural lands of Castilla y León and none (as far as I could see) in what appears to be similar habitat in the Guadalquivir valley. I remembered having read of a dramatic decrease in the number of storks in a region of Poland, which they attribute to the increased use of pesticides in recent years, and I wondered if this might be a factor here, the hotter, more humid climate of the Guadalquivir valley possibly necessitating greater use of pesticides than on the *meseta*.

Round the corner from the Plaza de San Fernando is an impressive market square enclosed by a colonnaded arcade. Along the narrow streets leading up to the top end of the city are some fine old mansions and several churches and convents. One of the mansions, the Lasso de la Vega Palacio, has recently been converted into a luxury hotel, the Casa de Carmona. We both needed to use a toilet and thought this would be as good a place as any, and better than most. We walked through public rooms exquisitely decorated and sumptuously furnished, but the room we had really gone to see had an 'out of order' notice on the door.

The city ends abruptly at a Roman gateway, the Puerta de Córdoba, situated at the north-east corner of the city, beyond which the road drops steeply to the plain below. An almost vertical rock face extends from this gateway to the Puerta de Sevilla in the west, and perched on the edge between the two, with a stunning view to the south across the endless plain, is the *parador*, built in the ruins of the 14th-century palace of King Pedro of Castile (Pedro The Cruel), which in turn was built within a Moorish castle.

Further evidence of Carmona's importance during Roman times lies in a large necropolis that was discovered in 1881 about

Puerta de Córdoba, Carmona

a quarter of a mile west of the Puerta de Sevilla containing nearly 1000 family tombs, many in subterranean chambers. Unfortunately the necropolis, and the churches, were closed in the evening, so after a selection of good *raciónes* in the Bar Plaza in the Plaza de San Fernando we strolled aimlessly through the maze of narrow and now almost deserted streets. Suddenly our ears pricked up at the faint sound of music in the distance. We hurried towards its source and soon located it in a small bar. Six men were sitting in a circle, two of them strumming guitars, another thumping off-beat rhythm on a wooden box held between his knees, and all of them singing loudly. A small group of young Germans looked on curiously. This was traditional *flamenco*, the men singing in unison accompanied by frantic off-beat hand-clapping, the intensity and passion of their singing reflected in contorted facial expressions, breaks between phrases punctuated by cries of *'olé'* from a few locals standing at the bar; I threw in a few *olés* of my own, somewhat to their surprise. The owner of the bar was their leader and later he told me that they were a semi-professional group and had got together to rehearse. We were lucky to be treated to such entertainment for the price of a couple of brandies. It could have been for free because I walked out absentmindedly without paying; when I realized and returned half an hour later he said *"no hay problema"* and offered me another brandy on the house. He clearly was more interested in his music than in making money that evening.

Flamenco, expressed in dancing as well as in singing, is ingrained in Spanish gypsy culture. Its origin is uncertain but it is most likely to have evolved from Arabic music during the long years of Moorish rule, gradually absorbing more modern influences. Its heartland is in Andalucía where it is the music of the people (a radio station appropriately named Radio Olé treats its listeners to many hours of *flamenco* every day), but it also has wide appeal in other parts of Spain. Traditional folk music in Britain (and, I suspect, in other northern European countries) is prevented from dying out completely only by small groups of enthusiasts, but it has negligible general appeal; in Spain *flamenco* is alive and well. It is, however, not the sort of music that falls easily on the ears of most non-Spaniards — Roger, for example, was interested rather than entertained. The singers do not aspire to produce smooth and pure tones; their voices are rough, raucous and loud, but they emanate from deep within their hearts, passionate in expressing profound feelings of love, hate, hope, despair, sadness, and even, occasionally, of happiness. I like most kinds of music but *flamenco*, even without understanding most of the lyrics, stirs in me the sort of excitement that I get from traditional jazz, excitement that is given vent in *flamenco* by intermittent cries of "*olé*" and in jazz by applause and shouts of "yeah" following an inspiring solo break. Both types of music force an active response from all but the most disinterested listener.

Back at our *pensión*, Antonio, mercifully, had run out of steam, and peace and quiet reigned.

CHAPTER 13
HOT AND BOTHERED
CARMONA TO EL CUERVO

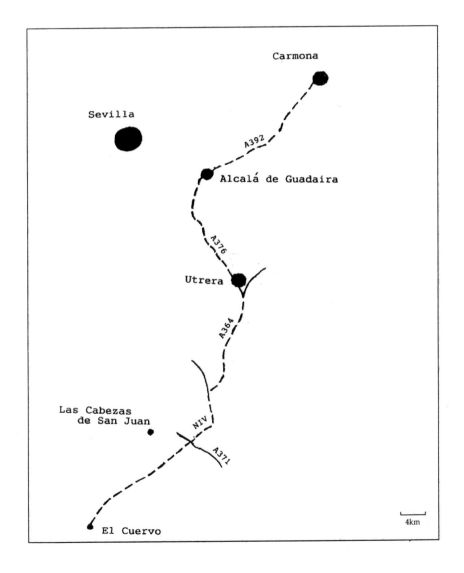

The general plan next day was to head towards Arcos de la Frontera, but the best route was not obvious. We decided to take the minor roads through Alcalá de Guadaira to Utrera, and there pick up the main road south. I don't know if a different route would have been better, but this one as far as Utrera was dreadful. It was the first time we had encountered bad roads: narrow and rough, the slow lane in particular potholed and strewn with stones. Traffic was heavy and if we dared stray out of our lane on to the rather smoother road we risked being bumped off by truck drivers who clearly felt that cyclists out of their lane were fair game.

The main road skirts round Utrera but by mistake we found ourselves on a wide cobbled street leading to the centre. It was market day and the place was throbbing with activity. I rested on the steps of a large covered food market, keeping an eye on the bicycles while Roger went inside to buy some fruit. I must have looked tired because an elderly gentleman offered me the chair he was sitting on; it was kind of him, but I have not yet reached the stage in life when I feel I can take advantage of such a gesture, especially when it comes from someone even older than myself. On the move again we threaded our way carefully between street stalls offering anything from clothing and furniture to jewelry and pots and pans. The stalls were so tightly packed that progress was slow and mostly on foot, with the calls of the stall-holders, some of whom were tall, black Africans in colourful robes, ringing in our ears.

We emerged from the bustle of Utrera to join the A364, a much better road than that on which we had entered. About 18km further south the traffic became even heavier on joining the NIV, the main road to Jerez de la Frontera, Cádiz and all points south, but now the wide and smooth slow lane provided welcome sanctuary from the monster trucks thundering by.

We paused for a drink in an isolated bar at a crossroads 9km further on. It proved also to be a crossroads in a different sense: it marked the spot where the first major disagreement occurred within the *Viejo Equipo*. I wanted to continue towards Arcos de la Frontera, taking a left turn at the crossroads on to the minor road A371. Roger, on the other hand, was now wary of minor roads in

Andalucía, suspecting that they were not up to the standard of the minor roads we had found elsewhere, and therefore he wanted to continue on the main road. Also, for the first time, he announced that he would like to go to Sanlúcar de Barrameda on the coast, and cross the Guadalquivir estuary to visit the famous Cota Doñana national park. This was a reasonable idea but it involved a considerable detour from the most direct route south. I was already beginning to visualize and long for the moment when we would cross the finishing line into Gibraltar, and did not want to ride even a kilometer farther than was necessary to reach that goal. The challenge we had taken on was hard enough for me: I could see no reason for making it harder. There, in that lonely bar in the middle of nowhere, the argument was pursued to and fro until it was finally resolved — and we headed down the main road, destination Sanlúcar de Barrameda. Well, he was the team captain! What tipped the balance in my mind, apart from the need to humour the man, was the fact that it was quite hot and getting hotter every day, and I persuaded myself that fresh sea air would be welcome.

We had already cycled nearly 80km. Although the terrain was relatively flat compared with much of what had gone before, the heat made the going tough and I had had about enough. The only town or village marked on the map as being on the road was El Cuervo, 21km away, and it was with some relief that I saw the sign of Venta Manolo by the roadside as we approached the town. It is a large *venta*, with a spacious bar and restaurant and, more importantly, rooms to let. Having at last learned from previous experiences, I made sure I was given a room at the back, and there the process of recuperation began, completed later with a good meal in the *venta* watching yet another football match. The *venta* is slightly outside the town and we could not summon up the energy or enthusiasm to go out and explore it. What delights may we have missed?

CHAPTER 14
FIGHTING THE LEVANTE

El Cuervo to Chipiona

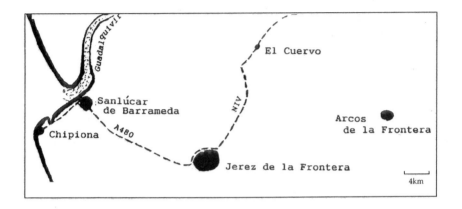

The first thing I heard on waking next morning was a strong wind whistling through the trees. At breakfast we were told it was the *levante*, the east wind, so we thought this might actually help us, since we were travelling in a south-westerly direction. However, out on the road we found it was hitting us head-on or broadsides; it must have been a south-easterly, and swirling northwards. The wind was to plague us for the next two days. Every yard had to be fought for. Many hills we had encountered on our journey had presented reasonable tests of our resolve but now even small gradients felt like mountains. It was hot, the traffic was heavy, the going was tough, and negative thoughts began to creep into my mind: "What was I doing here?", "Why hadn't I ignored Roger's stupid challenge?". I humoured myself by singing jazz tunes out loud, keeping beat with each turn of the pedals. At that time I wished I was blowing my trumpet with my jazz band in Bristol instead of slogging away on a bicycle in Andalucía. Against the wind it was a struggle to keep up with the beat of even slow blues numbers like St James Infirmary or Buddy Bolden Blues.

We had both been to Jerez de la Frontera on previous visits to Spain so we skirted round it on the main road. Then we turned north-west towards Sanlúcar de Barrameda and suddenly the wind was behind us. Like yachts turning downwind and raising their spinnakers we flew down the road, and fast numbers such as The Sheik of Araby and Dr Jazz replaced the blues.

Sanlúcar de Barrameda is a popular holiday resort at the mouth of the Gaudalquivir. It was the first of May, a public holiday; the *paseo maritimo* (beachfront promenade) was bustling with activity and the cafés and restaurants were crowded. It has always been a busy fishing port but there is also an upper part of the town, on a hill overlooking the river, which has been more concerned with agriculture than with fishing. On the hill stands an 11th-century Moorish palace, which became the home of successive dukes of Medina Sidonia, for many centuries among the biggest landowners in Spain. Sanlúcar is also well known as the centre for *manzanilla*, a very popular pale dry sherry.

During the 16th and early 17th centuries Seville was the major Spanish port for trade with the Americas, but from the middle of the 17th century the Guadalquivir became increasingly difficult to navigate as far as Seville, and other ports, such as Sanlúcar and, especially, Cádiz, gained in importance. Columbus sailed from Sanlúcar in 1498 returning to his ill-fated colony on the island of Hispañola, and Francisco Pizarro also, in 1529, on his way to Panama and thence to conquer Peru. But the most memorable day in the history of the port must be September 6 1522 when a small ship called the *Victoria* limped into the harbour. Three years earlier, on September 20 1519, she had sailed out of the same harbour under the command of Ferdinand Magellan, a Portuguese then in the service of Spain. The *Victoria* was one of a fleet of five ships, none more than 130 tons, that set out with a total of 260 men in search of a western route to the Pacific Ocean and the riches of the east. She is famous not only for having taken Magellan through the strait that now bears his name but also for having continued westwards and been the first ship to circumnavigate the globe. Magellan, sadly, was killed fighting the natives in the Philippine island of Mactan, but the *Victoria*, the only survivor of the original fleet, was brought home, albeit in a battered state and with only 17 of the original 50 men on board.

Roger investigated the possibility of crossing to the Cota Doñana national park on the opposite bank of the river, but groups are taken over for guided tours only twice a day and the timing was inconvenient; it appeared, moreover, that the tours allow only very superficial exploration of the park. After lunch in one of the promenade restaurants we were on the road again, heading west to Chipiona, another popular resort situated where the coastline from Sanlúcar turns south, the town looking out to sea over wonderful beaches to the north and west. Unfortunately the wind was still howling and it was not a day to enjoy a beach.

We had already noticed an abnormally large number of motorbikes on the roads, and now they all seemed to have come to roost in Chipiona. Parked outside every hotel, *hostal* and *pensión* there was an assortment of powerful machines, and, worse still, their riders had taken up all the rooms. Up to this point on our journey we had experienced no problems finding accommodation, but here it was only after trying about six establishments that we were able to find a room — and it was only one room. Roger would have to risk being disturbed by my snoring and I would have to risk being shaken up by his violent ripostes, all of which had been avoided since the turbulent night in Toro.

Chipiona's bars were buzzing with lively groups of attractive young people, which made a nice change from the rather drab clientele generally to be found in bars out in 'the sticks'. Most were weekend escapees from the big cities, but many, no doubt, were bikers and their pillion-riding friends, unrecognizable as such out of their leathers. We had by that time learned that the reason for the invasion of motorbikes was that the Spanish Grand Prix takes place in Jerez de la Frontera each year on the Sunday of this May Day weekend and that enthusiasts descend on the area from all over Europe for reunions prior to the race. We made our way down the *calle peatón* (pedestrian street) to the north-facing promenade and there enjoyed *raciónes* of fresh fish in the Bar Trebujena — not surprisingly, fish is abundant in these parts.

Returning to our *hostal* I had a brilliant idea: I removed the mattress from my bed and jammed it into the small bathroom, preferring to risk being trampled on (or worse) during the night should Roger use the toilet to being physically assaulted each time I disturbed his sleep. There was a risk that the bathroom's acoustics might amplify the snores and provoke even fiercer retaliation, but I felt my first priority was to place myself beyond the range of direct attack. It worked well.

CHAPTER 15
MORE LEVANTE BLUES
CHIPIONA TO SAN FERNANDO

The wind was blowing even more strongly next morning. We decided to go out and fight it but to aim only to reach El Puerto de Santa Maria, 42km away. Even in the lowest gears it was a real struggle to make any headway, pedals revolving no faster than the slowest blues beat. The road makes a loop of about 15km round the US naval base at Rota before reaching El Puerto. We pulled in to a small bar on the long straight road into the town. It was early afternoon and five or six middle-aged men were sitting around small tables in jovial mood, drinking the local *manzanilla*. We had already managed to establish friendly rapport with them — to the extent of exchanging rounds of drinks — when the star of the day, wearing bright green overalls, entered the bar. He was tall, slim, had jet black hair and wore thick black-rimmed spectacles. He immediately reminded me of that great comedian, the late Eric Morecambe, and he was certainly the comedian in that bar. He took centre stage, standing with his back to the bar, facing his friends who lost no time in provoking him with friendly insults and innuendos, only some of which did we understand. The atmosphere, which had been happy enough before he came, was transformed into one of raucous hilarity, roars of laughter bursting out as first one and then another scored points off each other. Not only did our comedian have the best punch lines but his gestures and facial expressions were in themselves hilarious. We gathered that he was one of the town's roadsweepers and when he was challenged to explain why he was in the bar at that time of day instead of out cleaning the streets he went on to describe, in graphic detail and with appropriate body language, all the different types of human and animal waste he had picked up that day and to claim that the streets of the entire neighbourhood were now squeaky clean. I asked him what the letters on his overalls stood for and he replied that they spelt out the German word for *mierda* (shit), which was not relevant to my question but which he must have thought was a more interesting answer. He then wanted to know the English word for *mierda*, after which, individually or in unison, they all tried vainly to pronounce it. Listening to these men repeatedly shouting out "sheet" amid howls of laughter was a side-splitting experience.

All this was much more fun than fighting against the wind on a busy road, but if we had stayed much longer we would not have been capable of riding at all. Reluctantly we took our leave, despite their efforts to buy us more beer. We were thinking of staying in the town, which is famous for its fish restaurants, but as we cycled through the town we saw that the motorbikers were there in force. The *plazas* were chock-full of parked bikes, looking like swarms of beetles, their riders filling the cafés around the *plazas*. This was no place for us or our pedal-powered machines, so we carried on, leaving town on the NIV. But we could not get away from them. There on the main road they roared up and down at high speed (normal speed regulations seemed to have been suspended during this weekend), many of them demonstrating their 'wheely' skills, the traditional race winner's celebration stunt of lifting the bike almost vertical on its rear wheel. These exhibitions of power and speed made me feel very small and insignificant, grinding away as I was at snail's pace. At that time I would gladly have exchanged bikes with one of them.

We soon pulled in to Valdelagrana, a resort on the beach, in the hope of finding accommodation there, but again those wretched machines were parked outside every hotel — even a large 10-storey hotel was full. So on we went. Looping round on a flyover to cross the A4 *autopista* near Puerto Real the wind bore down on us broadside so strongly that we had to dismount for fear of being blown off. Resuming in a south-easterly direction after crossing the *autopista* I consoled myself with the thought that hard as it had been over the last couple of days against the headwind it would have been even harder, or even impossible, had it been a crosswind. We considered trying our luck in Puerto Real but the road by-passes the town so we carried on. Then, about 6km further on, approaching San Fernando, a most welcome sight loomed up on the left: the Hostal El Pinar. Again there were motorbikes outside, but only three of them — there was hope. The landlady at first said she had no rooms available, but seeing how far my face dropped said there was one with a broken door. Without hesitation I snapped it up. Roger, amazingly finding a surplus reserve of energy, wanted to carry on to San Fernando, but on this occasion I used my veto. I had to agree that

Motorbikes again — here at Hostal El Pinar

El Toro — in the past an advertisement for a Spanish brandy, now a feature of the Andalucian landscape

the Hostal El Pinar was not a particularly exciting establishment, but I had struggled enough and any place with a bed would do for me. The room, which was off a courtyard at the back, was in fact a suite of two rooms (bedroom and sitting room) and a large bathroom. The little matter of a broken door could easily be overlooked. The sofa in the sitting room had a pull-out bed so I was able to get away from Roger, this time without sleeping in the bathroom.

We were served a simple but acceptable meal with a cheap and awful *vino de la casa* (probably a homemade *manzanilla*) while being subjected by television not to another football match but to a beaming Tony Blair after his crushing election victory. Later we met the bikers in the bar. They were Dutch and had come down for the long weekend. They confirmed that this was a popular annual jamboree for bikers from all over Europe. The world championship race held in Jerez on the Sunday is the big draw but socializing with fellow bikers before and during the event is an important part of the fun. Fun for them, I'm sure, but for anyone else it is a time to give the whole area a wide berth. Late into the night and into the early hours powerful machines sped up and down the main road like demented wasps.

What had been intended on leaving Chipiona to be a short hop, because of the difficult conditions, to El Puerto de Santa Maria, had become a longer one of about 60km and, apart from the afternoon's hilarious interlude in the Puerto bar, it had been the least enjoyable day of the trip so far. (This last statement is the sort of gross understatement for which the British are famous.)

CHAPTER 16
REST-CURE IN CONIL

SAN FERNANDO TO CONIL DE LA FRONTERA

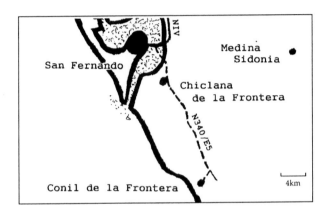

On waking next morning my ears immediately pricked up to listen for the wind. I lay there for some time not daring to believe that I could not hear it. But it was true: the wind that had blighted our lives for two days had died down. It was a perfect sunny day. After about 5km we finally left the horrendously busy NIV and joined the quieter N340/E5. We could have reached, or at least got close to, Gibraltar on the same day, but we still had four days in hand before our arranged rendezvous, so we decided that what we should do is find a pleasant place on a beach and take it easy for a couple of days. With this in mind we turned off the road towards the coast to have a look at Conil de la Frontera

We could not have stumbled on a better place. It is a small whitewashed town situated on a magnificent wide sandy beach that stretches almost uninterrupted from Cádiz in the north to Tarifa in the south, a distance of about 90km. Although the town has expanded greatly since it was a small fishing village, old buildings on narrow streets near the beach retain their timeless character. Along a pedestrianized section we found the Pensión Torre de Guzman, a charming place with a simple but attractive open *patio* full of colourful plants in pots, and creepers up the walls. They could only offer us a double room, but the place was so pleasant that we accepted it, even though it might condemn me to another night on the bathroom floor.

The beach, just a couple of hundred yards down the road from the *pensión*, beckoned strongly. Although it was a beautiful sunny day and a Sunday, we had the beach almost to ourselves. We saw no tourists, and few Spaniards head for their beaches so early in the year. But the beach, more than 100 yards from promenade to sea and stretching north and south as far as the eye can see, would still have been uncrowded if the 16,000 inhabitants of Conil had descended upon it. After a sleep on the soft yellow sand and a late lunch of grilled *salmonetes* (red mullet) in the beachfront Bar Bahia, I spent the afternoon strolling up and down the beach, stopping from time to time for a dip in the cool sea, then lying down for another nap. This is the life, I thought. What a contrast from the exertions of the previous few days.

Rested but somewhat dazed after several hours' exposure to the sun, we ambled slowly back to our *pensión*, passing the 16th-

Conil de la Frontera —
entrance to the old part of town,
and the beach

century Torre de Guzman (Guzman's tower). Don Alfonso Perez de Guzman, or Guzman El Bueno (The Good) is famous in Spanish history for his defiance and personal sacrifice in defence of Tarifa against the Moors in 1294. The town had been captured from the Moors two years earlier by Sancho IV El Bravo (The Brave), King of Castile, but his brother Juan turned traitor to help the Moors recover it. He had Guzman's 9-year-old son as a page in his retinue, and he used the boy as a hostage, demanding surrender of the town in exchange for the boy's life. Guzman is recorded as having chosen "honour without a son to a son with dishonour", and, in a final defiant gesture, to have thrown his sword down from the castle walls for the execution. Among the rewards heaped on Guzman by King Sancho was the Conil tuna-fishing industry, and later (in 1299) the town itself was granted to him by Sancho's heir, Fernando IV. The town and the whole region were then, for over 500 years until they were declared Crown property, the domain of Guzman's descendants, the dukes of Medina Sidonia, the incumbent in 1588 being the reluctant and ill-fated leader of the Spanish Armada. The tower, standing about 100 feet high, has been well restored and now stands in a small enclosure by the side of the street that leads to the beach.

There are some hotels and *hostales* in the town, reflecting the unsurprising fact that it is a popular place during the summer months. The town provides most of the basic amenities such as a bank, a post office, a few small shops and, of course, cafés, bars and restaurants (Roger even found somewhere from where to send a fax), but it has not yet been spoilt by overdevelopment. A partially constructed tiled beachfront promenade suggested a desire for further development but it appeared to have been abandoned in its unfinished state as if the town was still uncertain whether it wants to develop into a grand tourist resort. We liked it as we found it, simple and unsophisticated.

Wandering around the town in the evening we met a young German couple in a bar on the modest Plaza de España. They were in love with the town and the whole region. They had given up their jobs and sold their house in Germany and had now settled in the country outside Conil where they were developing an equestrian centre, horses and horseriding being their passion in life. For them this region is close to paradise: wonderful beaches, unspoilt towns and pleasant open country gently rising to the foothills of the great Andalucian sierras. Despite all its attributes the coast, known as the Costa de la Luz, has not developed like, for example, the Costa del Sol on the Mediterranean coast past Gibraltar, the main reason being that it is exposed to the more unpredictable and sometimes wild Atlantic weather.

We still had days to spare before our rendezvous in Gibraltar, so we decided that we could treat ourselves to another full day in Conil. After an undisturbed night's sleep (rearranging the bedroom furniture so as to separate the two beds as far as possible made it unnecessary on this occasion for me to sleep on the bathroom floor) I woke late to find the sun streaming into the room from clear blue skies, presaging another idyllic day of total relaxation ahead: a leisurely breakfast in our *patio*, loafing on the beach, cooling off occasionally with a swim, a seafood lunch, *siesta* on the warm sand. I daresay one could get bored with such a lifestyle but as a rest-cure it is hard to beat.

Gazing out to sea I tried to recall famous historical events that had taken place out there. To the right, about 30km up the coast, was Cádiz, and to the left, only 15km away, Cape Trafalgar, places that brought to mind Francis Drake's audacious raid on Spanish shipping in Cádiz harbour in 1587 and Nelson's famous victory in the Battle of Trafalgar in 1805. Drake boasted of "singeing the King of Spain's beard", and he certainly caused Felipe II some discomfort by forcing a considerable delay in the sailing of the Spanish Armada. Felipe wanted it to sail by the summer of 1587, but Drake's raid on the 24th of April destroyed so many of his ships that it did not set out until 30 May 1588. The Spanish fleet was being assembled in Lisbon, and Queen Elizabeth's orders to Drake were to do everything possible to obstruct this, even if it meant "distressing their ships within their harbours". On 2 April Drake sailed from Plymouth with a fleet of 23 ships, to which the Queen had contributed six, four of them galleons (including the flagship *Elizabeth Bonaventure*). About a week later an amended and contradictory order was announced: "You shall forbear to enter forcibly into any of the said king's ports or havens, or to offer violence to any of his towns or shipping within harbouring, or to do any act of hostility upon the land". Whether this order indicated a genuine change of mind is uncertain; it is possible that the Queen wished to place total responsibility on Drake for any action he might take, thus absolving herself and not compromising further her uneasy relationship with the king of Spain. On his way down the Portuguese coast Drake heard from passing Flemish merchant ships that Cádiz harbour was full of Spanish ships and, not surprisingly, he wasted no time getting there. His fleet swept into the harbour at 4 o'clock in the afternoon of 19 April and proceeded to attack the surprised Spaniards incessantly throughout the evening and the following day. According to Drake 37 Spanish ships were destroyed (24 according to the Spaniards), among them the great galleon belonging to the Marquis de Santa Cruz, who was to have led the Armada but who died in February 1588. The din of battle must have been heard in Conil.

The Battle of Trafalgar, which took place over 200 years later, on 21 October, 1805, was the most important naval battle of the Napoleonic Wars and, indeed, one of the most famous and significant battles in British history, marked by the tragic death of our greatest naval hero, Admiral Horatio Nelson. A series of important events during the previous 6 months led up to the battle. Napoleon had been threatening to invade England since the summer of 1803. By March 1805 his enormous Army of England (later called La Grande Armée) of over 100,000 men lay ready and waiting in camps around Boulogne, and a huge flotilla of shallow-draught ships and landing craft had been specially built to carry them, their horses, guns and supplies across. The only problem for Napoleon was how to cross the Channel when the British controlled the seas. The French navy was dispersed in Toulon, Brest and Rochefort and somehow he had to gather the three squadrons together into a combined fleet capable of competing with the British in the Channel. He entreated his admirals to "make us masters of the Channel for three days and we are masters of the world". His plan was for the three squadrons to rendezvous in the West Indies and for the combined fleet to sail together to the Channel. But the plan did not materialise. The

Brest squadron under Admiral Gauteaume could not break out of port because of Admiral Cornwallis's blockade, and the Rochefort squadron under Admiral Missiessy, which did reach the West Indies, turned back after two months' waiting for his colleagues. The Toulon squadron under Admiral Villeneuve eventually broke out with 11 ships from a constant two-year blockade by Nelson and, with six Spanish ships that joined him in Cádiz, reached the West Indies. Nelson, with 10 ships, pursued him on his fruitless journey and then back again across the Atlantic where Villeneuve tried, in vain, to link up with the Brest squadron and with a French/Spanish squadron based in Ferrol. With the failure to gather together a combined fleet the invasion threat to England evaporated and Villeneuve took refuge in Cádiz. Napoleon turned his attention elsewhere and in August 1805 marched his huge army from Boulogne to fight the Austrians on the Danube. He ordered Villeneuve to sail east to support his planned exploits in the Mediterranean and this set the stage for the great battle off Cape Trafalgar. Anyone sitting on the Conil beach on 21 October 1805 would have had a grandstand view. Nelson's fleet was lying out of sight about 10 miles out to sea, ready to pounce. The French left port on 19 October and headed south towards the Strait of Gibraltar. The British advanced on them from the south in two columns, one headed by Nelson on *Victory* and the other by Admiral Collingwood on *Royal Sovereign*. Lined up against the British fleet of 27 ships were 27 French ships under Villeneuve and 12 Spanish ships under Admiral Gravina. Hostilities began off Cape Trafalgar at noon on 21 October and by 4.30 it was all over. Twenty-two enemy ships were lost and it was a decisive British victory. But the great Admiral Nelson was dead. *Victory* had sailed between and engaged two French ships, the flagship *Bucentaure* and the *Redoutable*, and at about 1.30pm Nelson was hit by a bullet shot from the masthead of the *Redoutable*. The *Victory*'s log recorded: "Partial firing continued until 4.30 when a victory having been reported to the Right Honorable Lord Viscount Nelson, K.B. and Commander-in-Chief, he then died of his wound".

CHAPTER 17
THE TOE OF IBERIA
CONIL DE LA FRONTERA TO TARIFA

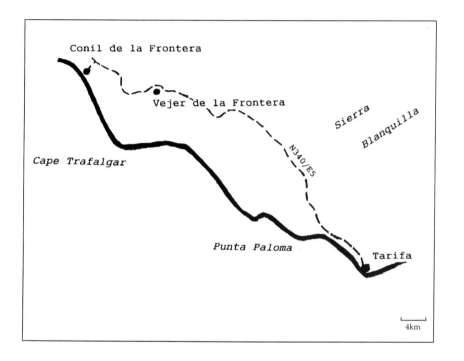

Somewhat reluctantly we left Conil the next day after a leisurely breakfast in our *patio*, which was disturbed only by Roger's insatiable need for mental stimulation, even first thing in the morning. Not for the first time he brought his Spanish grammar book to the breakfast table and proceeded to fire questions at me. My Spanish may be better than his but it is not based on a firm understanding of its grammar. Indeed I hardly know the difference between a preposition and a pronoun in English, let alone Spanish, so some of his questions remained unanswered. I was, however, useful in correcting his pronunciation, some of which was especially important to correct. For example, he insisted on accentuating the first instead of the second syllable of *conejo* (rabbit), making it sound dangerously like a common swear word that literally refers to a sensitive part of the female anatomy. I tried more than once in restaurants to persuade him to order rabbit so as to enjoy the waiter's reaction, but somehow he managed to avoid the trap.

Our stay at the Pensión Torre de Guzman had been extremely pleasant, in large measure due to the charming and obliging family who own it. The husband is the chef, the wife is the housekeeper and gardener, the two sons serve the bar and the adjoining *heladeria*, and a young daughter smiles happily in the background. They bought the old house about 12 years ago and have gradually developed it into a thriving family business.

Our next destination was Tarifa, only 65km down the N340. It was an easy ride, made even easier by a westerly breeze. The road by-passes Vejer de la Frontera 13km from Conil, the town perched on a hill high above the road. It would have been a hard climb up to the town (I'm sure even Roger would have had to walk), so we carried on, but I know from a previous visit that it is a fascinating old town, a maze of narrow streets between old whitewashed houses opening up here and there into small leafy *plazas*, and at its fringes superb views across the surrounding countryside. Further on, the coast past Punta Paloma is the domain of windsurfers, who flock to it from all parts of Europe to test their skills against westerlies blowing in from the Atlantic or easterlies rushing through the Strait of Gibraltar. We turned off the road a few kilometres short of Tarifa, down a short track between pine trees to the Hostal Millón situated on the beach facing the north African coast, which was only about 10km away but hardly visible through a hazy mist. Surfboards and sails lay on a small lawn in front of the *hostal*, their owners having a midday break or perhaps waiting for a more challenging wind. The beach extends south as far as Tarifa, and somewhere along it the Moors made their first landing in Spain, in AD710. Musa ibn Nasayr, the commander who had led the Arab army across north Africa to what is now Morocco, sent Tarif abn Zarah with a small force of Berbers (the native Moroccans) on a reconnaisance mission from Tangier. The definitive invasion of Spain by a much larger force was made elsewhere the following year.

After devouring a large plateful of succulent grilled sardines at the Hostal Millón, we headed for Tarifa. Although Gibraltar was our ultimate destination, Tarifa is the most southerly point in Europe and therefore, strictly speaking, the end-point of our trans-Iberian challenge. We cycled down the *alameda* to the harbour and then to the very end of the wharf that juts out to sea. This was it: we'd made it, mission accomplished. We could go no further without slipping into the sea. Alone on the wharf we quietly congratulated ourselves. It would have been nice to open a bottle of champagne (and drink it, not spray it all about as racing drivers stupidly do) but instead I was reminded of Robert Louis Stevenson's famous statement: "To travel hopefully is better than to arrive, and the true success is to labour". We had certainly laboured (before our rest in Conil) and our reward was to be standing there looking out across the calm waters of the Strait to the Moroccan coastline and the Rif mountains, now clearer behind the lifting mist, the white buildings of Tangier visible under a cloudless sky and the Tarifa fishing boats returning home after their day's toil. Even without the champagne these were moments to savour.

Tarifa was to serve the Moors well for over 500 years, being the main port through which they supplied their armies for the conquest of Spain and for many years thereafter, and also the base from which they controlled and levied dues on shipping passing through the Strait, giving rise to our word 'tariff'. It was not until 1292 that Sancho IV captured Tarifa from the Moors.

125

Outside Hostal Millón, Moroccan coast in background

Looking across the Strait of Gibraltar from Tarifa wharf

Two years later, Guzman's heroic defence resisted the inevitable Moorish siege.

Another important battle was waged here during the Napoleonic Wars. The French had conquered most of Andalucía but their Marshal Soult dearly wanted to have Tarifa as a port through which to receive supplies from Morocco. From 29 December 1811 to 5 January 1812 a large French force of about 10,000 men was successfully repulsed by a small Spanish garrison under General Copons supported by a few hundred British soldiers sent up from Gibraltar. The French succeeded in making a wide breach in the old Moorish wall but heavy fire from both sides coupled with torrential rain hampered their advance and eventually forced them to withdraw.

We booked into the Hostal Alameda at the lower end of the *alameda* gardens. This was the sixteenth *hostal* or *pensión* we had stayed in on the trip, and there is not one that we did not rate as perfectly satisfactory. For travellers who simply want a bed for the night this class of accommodation is more than adequate, and cheap — we never paid more than 3000 pesetas (about £12) for a single room, or 5000 pesetas (about £20) on the few occasions when we had no alternative but to accept a double room. The rooms are clean and most have *en suite* bathrooms. Constant features of the rooms are the long sausage-shaped pillows (which would make excellent weapons for a pillow fight, one game that Roger, thankfully, had grown out of), and the use of sheets and blankets rather than the duvets that have become so popular elsewhere in Europe. I can appreciate that not having to place and tuck in sheets and blankets can make duvets popular with those who make the beds, but why they should be popular with those who sleep under them amazes me. My experience is of body temperature first rising to boiling point and then, after pulling back the duvet, dropping uncomfortably low. Repeated cycles of heat and cold make for a restless night. Surely it is more sensible to have a few layers of cover that can be peeled off one by one according to need — but this simple logic is stubbornly dismissed by duvet-lovers. Interesting features of many of their bathrooms include the absence of bath plugs and the unfriendly design of their wash basins. World travellers have long reported that a personal bath plug is an essential item of equipment, and Roger's daughter had given him the one she had carried for six months around the world. He managed to lose it by the third day. The basin design is such that the simple procedure of washing one's face must be carried out with care. Instead of hot and cold water passing through separate taps, they are brought together through a single central outlet high above the basin, precisely in the path of one's head as it is lowered over it. On one occasion not only did I bang my forehead on the outlet but, on recoiling from the blow, hit the back of my head against a glass shelf fitted low above the basin, sending the shelf and everything on it crashing to the floor.

Roger resumed his relentless search for fax machines and postcards while I walked down to the Puerto de Pescadores (the fishermen's port) on the opposite side of the harbour from where we had stood earlier in the day. The fishermen had deposited their catches in a huge shed where an auction was in progress, the calls of the auctioneer echoing noisily around the building. Later I strolled into the town, bought a couple of huge cream cakes at a *pasteleria* and sat at a café to devour them with a cup of tea. *Pastelerias* offer a mouth-watering selection of cakes and pastries but, strangely, give customers little or no encouragement to eat them on the premises. Many do not even provide anywhere to sit, nor do they serve coffee or tea, which many people would choose to drink with a cake or pastry. It seems to be assumed that customers will take their *pasteles* to a café or take them home — or, indeed, eat them 'on the hoof'. This was the first time on this trip that I had ordered a cup of tea, and it reminded me that British travellers in Spain will not often enjoy what they consider to be 'a nice cup of tea'. *Té* in a Spanish café or bar is simply a cup of hot water and a tea bag, and milk is not provided unless requested. Spaniards are not great tea drinkers and often prefer other infusions like *manzanilla* (camomile) — not to be confused with *manzanilla* sherry — or *poleo* (peppermint), which also are generally available in cafés and bars.

Roger, having completed his important business, joined me at the café. We walked to the castle, which is named after Guzman El Bueno, but found it closed. By the road outside the castle entrance is a statue of Sancho IV El Bravo.

Dining in the restaurant below our *hostal* we reflected on how utterly predictable are the menus in most run-of-the-mill restaurants in Spain. There are always a few starters, usually including various *sopas* (soups) like *gazpacho* (cold vegetable soup), *sopa de pescado* or *de mariscos* (fish or shellfish soup), *huevos* or *esparrago con mayonesa* (egg or asparagus with mayonnaise), *jamon ibérico* (cured ham) and *salada mixta* (mixed salad with tuna, cheese and olives). For the main course there is usually a long list of different fish (not all available on the day) and meat, each offered either fried or grilled and served with a few chips but no other vegetables. Deserts are strictly limited, often just *flan* (*crème caramel*) or *helado* (ice cream). This simple fare is satisfying and very good value: it is not unusual to find 3-course menus, including bread and a bottle of wine, offered at 800-1000 pesetas (about £4). British travellers who are wary of food in foreign countries (and there are many who are) need have no worries in Spain, although they might be disappointed by the small portions of chips normally served and by the lack of interesting deserts — such English delicacies as spotted dick and treacle pudding are unheard of. Then, of course, there are the *platos combinados*, often, rather curiously, advertised outside the bar with large colour photographs displaying huge platefuls of each of the combinations available, presumably to enable customers before they enter to make crucial decisions such as whether to have one egg or two, or sausage instead of bacon. An occasional addition to the standard menu, especially in rural areas, is a *cocido* (stew). I remember a *cocido de cerdo* (pork stew) we had somewhere between Trujillo and Mérida, and a *cocido de venado* (venison stew) in Constantina, both of which were excellent. More varied and imaginative dishes, including local specialities, can, of course, be found in more expensive restaurants. Especially popular in Castilla y León are *cochinillo asado* (roast suckling pig) and *lechazo asado* (roast suckling lamb), neither of which, I guess, would be popular with the average British traveller. I saw a *cochinillo* on a plate in a restaurant in Medina de Rioseco, a whole baby pig which can barely have emerged from its mother's womb, cut along its belly and opened up from snout to tail, lying on its front with head intact and legs splayed out on each side of the plate, its back an orange-brown crackling — the sort of sight to turn many a carnivore into a vegetarian.

CHAPTER 18
BIRD'S-EYE VIEW OF THE STRAIT
TARIFA TO SAN ROQUE

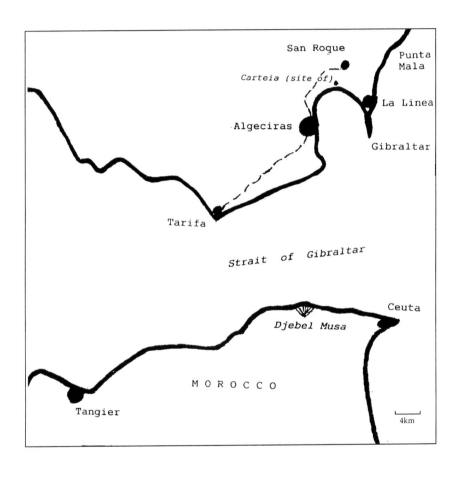

A final test awaited us next day: the long hill that climbs out of Tarifa in a north-easterly direction parallel to the coastline. I was fully prepared for a long walk but I set out in aggressive mood, determined to attack the hill. The westerly breeze was generally helpful but as the road zigzagged up the hill it was actually a hindrance at times. Soon I was down in my lowest gear, making very slow progress, only occasionally able to move up a gear and expecting at any moment to have to admit defeat and dismount. To my surprise, however, I did not feel seriously out of breath and my legs were still functioning, managing to maintain a steady blues beat, so I just kept going. Looking up the hill I kept hoping desperately that the next bend would mark the summit, only to have hopes dashed by the sight of yet another zigzag ahead. At last, to my relief and amazement, I reached the *mirador* (lookout) at the top. It had been a 9km climb and I felt quite pleased with myself, even more so when Roger (who had gone on ahead) admitted that he had walked part of the way. This really was a feather in my cap, the only one I had gained on the whole trip. So preoccupied had I been in my struggle up the hill that I had not admired the wonderful view, but now it was revealed in a fantastic panorama: wooded hillsides descending from the road to the sea, the coast of Morocco stretching from Ceuta in the east to Tangier in the west across the Strait of Gibraltar, and the Rif mountains beyond. Behind us, spaced out on the hilltops running down towards Tarifa, a long line of electricity-generating windmills was the only man-made intrusion into the wonderful landscape.

Beyond the *mirador* the road undulates for a few miles and then, suddenly, the Rock of Gibraltar began to appear like a mirage in the distance over the brow of a hill, first the outline of its crest and then, gradually as I rode up the hill, the whole Rock. At the top of the hill, on a bend in the road, the vista is stunning, the Rock framed perfectly between the branches of two trees across the wide sweep of the Bay of Gibraltar, a narrow peninsula jutting proudly out into the Strait, one of the two Pillars of Hercules. Approached from land, sea or air, the Rock is an imposing sight, dominant even in its spectacular setting. As a Gibraltarian, the first sight of it when returning after a long

First view of the Rock of Gibraltar

absence has always given me a special thrill, experienced many times as a boy returning home during school or university holidays. That same feeling was kindled again as I gazed out across the bay at the great Rock, the fitting final destination of our trip.

The Rock was only 25km away round the bay, but our agreed rendezvous there was not until the following day. Our plan was to stay overnight in San Roque, a town at the northern end of the bay where one of my daughters lived with her husband and young son. But first we were to pay a nostalgic visit to the Hotel Reina Cristina in Algeciras. Freewheeling for about 5km down the hill to Algeciras, and relaxing with a cool drink in the pleasant garden of the hotel, were just rewards for the hard slog up the hill from Tarifa. Up to about 30 years ago, when Algeciras was an attractive small town, the Reina Cristina was recognized as a top-class hotel for the discerning traveller, but since then the town has grown enormously and lost its charm, and the hotel now caters for the mass market of package tourism. In my youth, while on holiday in Gibraltar, it was the smartest place to take a girlfriend for a special night out, dining, wining and dancing in the moonlit garden to the romantic music of a small band. Now, tattooed and ear-ringed Brits were playing darts in the poolside bar and the advertised entertainment for the evening was bingo. It was sad to see the classy image of the hotel tarnished, but if it had not changed to cater for a different clientele it would almost certainly no longer exist — and would not have allowed two sweaty cyclists past its front door. It was good, however, to see that nothing much else has changed: the lounge area in the central internal *patio* is still an attractive and restful place and the buildings and gardens are well maintained. I took a nostalgic spin around the small dancefloor in the garden, arms outstreched as if holding a partner, reminiscing about exciting times there long ago — and looking a complete idiot, no doubt.

San Roque was only 13km away along a busy *autovia*. We arrived in mid-afternoon at my daughter's home at the top end of the town next to the church, and, adding to my pleasure, found my elder daughter, who lived in a nearby town, there too. My two thirtysomethings, both born in Bristol, were introduced to the region on various holidays during their childhood and have been drawn to live there by force of circumstance and by their love for the Mediterranean climate and lifestyle. It was a great moment falling into their arms at what was, to all intents and purposes, the end of our journey, before being subjected to the sort of analysis that daughters tend to inflict on their fathers: the scruffiness of my appearance and the white hair that had grown over my face came under particular scrutiny on this occasion. The last time I allowed my beard to grow, many years ago, it was bushy brown, but now it was snowy white. My wife had given me strict instructions not to turn up bearded in Gibraltar, so the lengthy ablutions that followed included the painful removal of all facial hair. The day ended in celebration and complete relaxation, Roger producing a bottle of champagne and my son-in-law producing fresh fish beautifully cooked on his barbecue.

San Roque has expanded considerably following the construction in the early 1970s of an oil refinery, a petrochemicals plant and other industries around the bay, but the central part is still fairly typical of a small Andalucian town: narrow cobbled streets, some buildings well maintained, with freshly white-washed walls, wrought-iron balconies and attractive internal *patios*, and some sadly delapidated. Its history is closely linked with that of Gibraltar. When a combined British and Dutch fleet under Admiral Sir George Rooke captured Gibraltar in 1704 most of the small Genoese community on the Rock decided to remain but most of the Spanish inhabitants fled to Spain, a large group settling around a hermitage in San Roque. Felipe V addressed the new settlement as "My city of Gibraltar resident in its Campo", and a large sign that now stands at the entrance to the town on the Malaga road carries the inscription 'La Ciudad de Gibraltar en San Roque'. No doubt the displaced population expected an early return to their homes in Gibraltar, but a succession of sieges, during which Spanish forces and their allies camped in and around San Roque, failed to dislodge the garrison. However, only 25 years after the end of the Great Siege of 1779-1783, when Napoleon was overrunning Spain, the situation was entirely different: instead of being the object of Spanish attacks, the Rock was a base supplying Spanish forces in Andalucía, and in 1810-1811 provided refuge for the people of San Roque while the French devastated their town. More recently, when Franco's army landed near Algeciras at the beginning of the Spanish Civil War in 1931, several thousand Spaniards from San Roque, Algeciras and other towns around the bay again took refuge in Gibraltar, where they were housed in temporary camps on the racecourse, now the airfield. The loss of Gibraltar in 1704 must have caused considerable distress to resident Spaniards who evacuated to San Roque and neighbouring towns, but their descendants have had reason, a few times in their history, to be grateful for the support of a British Gibraltar.

The oldest part of San Roque lies on the higher slopes of a hill, the church of Santa Maria La Coronada at its summit. From a *mirador* west of the church there is a magnificent view of the 10km-long and 7km-wide U-shaped bay, Gibraltar on the left, Algeciras on the right and the Moroccan coast in the distance, across the Strait. To enjoy the view, however, eyes must be kept firmly fixed on the far distance: dropping them reveals the smoking chimneys and awful grey buildings of the oil refinery and petrochemicals plant. Before the 1960s the entire shoreline was unspoilt, cork woods extending to beautiful beaches all along the bay. All this changed with industrial development of the area which was aimed, at least in part, at providing employment for Spaniards who increasingly were being prevented by their own government from working in Gibraltar, as part of their policy of exerting economic pressure on the Gibraltarians. In the early 1950s there were about 12,000 Spaniards commuting daily to Gibraltar; by the summer of 1969 there were only about 4500, and by the end of June 1969, when Spain finally isolated Gibraltar by closing the frontier and stopping the Algeciras ferry, there were none. How many Spaniards found permanent new employment is uncertain, but the scar on the landscape is permanent. Spain did not open the frontier again until 5 February 1985, having isolated the Rock for nearly 16 years, during which time the Gibraltarians could only leave their home by sea or air.

The Anglo-Dutch force that took Gibraltar in 1704 did so in support of the Hapsburg Archduke Charles of Austria during the War of the Spanish Succession, and in the terms of the truce that was agreed by Spain after a 4-day siege the Archduke was recognised as Carlos III of Spain. By this time, however, Philip of Anjou (grandson of Louis XIV of France) had succeeded to the throne as Felipe V, having been named as heir in the will of Carlos II, who died in 1700. A siege by a combined Spanish and French army lasting from September 1704 to April 1705 failed to dislodge the Gibraltar garrison under the command of Prince George of Hesse-Darmstadt, who had sailed to Gibraltar with Rooke. It was not until July 1713 that the war was ended by the Treaty of Utrecht in which Felipe V was accepted as King of Spain and Gibraltar was formally ceded to Britain.

Not surprisingly, Spain has been trying to recover the Rock ever since, despite the fact that the treaty states that Gibraltar was "to be held and enjoyed absolutely with all manner of right for ever, without any exception or impediment." However, since the treaty gave Spain first option on the Rock should Britain have no further use for it, and since the United Nations urges decolonisation of all remaining colonised territories around the world, Spain pursues her claim, ignoring a fundamental principle enshrined in the United Nations charter that colonised people should have the right to self-determination — a principle that the United Nations also chooses to ignore in this case. Gibraltarians would be pleased to discard the mantle of colonialism (nominal though this has been for many years) but on terms that recognises their right to a say in their future. In a referendum held on 10 September 1967, 12,038 Gibraltarians voted for continued association with Britain and only 44 for Spain, and if a referendum were held today there would be a similar result, despite the fact that Spain is now a democracy (albeit denying Gibraltarians fundamental democratic rights) whereas in 1968 it was still a fascist dictatorship. Despite such overwhelming rejection Spain continues to press her claim. Paul Theroux, in his book *The Pillars of Hercules*, opines that Gibraltarians "know that as sure as eggs are *huevos* the British will eventually hand them over to the King of Spain", but fortunately for Gibraltarians Britain has vowed, in the preamble to the current Gibraltar Constitution, not to cede sovereignty against the wishes of the Gibraltarians. The impasse remains, and continued Spanish economic and political pressure only makes Gibraltarians more hostile to their claim. The situation has been succinctly summarised by the late General Sir William Jackson, Governor of Gibraltar from 1978 to 1982, in the epilogue of his book *The Rock of the Gibraltarians*: ". . . the Anglo-Spanish dispute over Gibraltar is an argument about which is the more important: a large nation's claim to a small rocky peninsula attached to the southern coast of Iberia, or a small people's right to their home. In this penultimate decade of the twentieth century, in which humane policies have become the accepted norm, the people's right to their home must surely outweigh the territorial claim, based upon events that took place almost three hundred years ago. Good neighbourliness and mutual respect on both sides is all that really matters."

The tranquillity of the scene I was admiring from San Roque belied its often-turbulent past. The bay has been a great theatre in which history has been made over hundreds of years, with Moors, Spaniards and Britons playing the leading parts. The 'upper circle' on the San Roque hill would have provided a perfect view of all the drama. Immediately below, in the 'orchestra pit', almost completely lost among the chimneys, lie the remains of the town of Carteia, which was founded by the Phoenicians in about 940BC but which flourished and grew during nearly 600 years of Roman rule into a city with a population probably as great as a quarter of a million. It is hard to imagine this now, looking down from San Roque. It is through Carteia that Tarik ibn Ziyad is thought to have made his first attempt to invade Spain with an army of about 12,000 in AD711. The Visigoth commander Theodomir repulsed this attempt, but Tarik took his army round the Rock, landed somewhere on the Mediterranean coast between Gibraltar and Punta Mala, and then moved swiftly to capture Algeciras, Tarifa, Córdoba and Toledo. Tarik had been sent from North Africa by the senior Arab commander Musa ibn Nasayr, who then took over from Tarik at Toledo and in only 7 years conquered all but the north-west corner of Spain. Gibraltar derives its name from Tarik (Djebel Tarik, the mountain of Tarik), and the highest mountain on the Moroccan coast across the Strait, the southern Pillar of Hercules that forms the backcloth to the grand stage, is called Djebel Musa. (Some authors refer to Ceuta as the southern Pillar of Hercules, but on approaching by sea from the east as the ancient mariners did it is Musa not Ceuta that stands out with Gibraltar as the western gateway of the Mediterranean.)

For the next 600 years the bay staged no dramatic events as the area enjoyed peace in Moorish hands, but with the advance of the Christian *reconquista* conflict was bound to arise. The peace was shattered in 1309 as Djebel Tarik became Spanish for the first time since 711, and it was Guzman El Bueno, Governor of Tarifa since 1292, who was largely responsible. An army led by the Archbishop of Seville attacked from the north across the isthmus, while Guzman landed his force by sea on the sands south of the town, climbed up the Rock and besieged the Moorish castle (which stands at the north end of the town) from above. The next 200 years saw a succession of battles fought for control of the Rock. The Moors recaptured it in 1333 and resisted three Spanish sieges before being defeated in 1462 by a Spanish force led by Alonso de Arcos, the Governor of Tarifa. Alonso had help from the de Guzmans, who had by then become the feudal lords of much of south-west Spain, and Juan Alonso de Guzman, Guzman El Bueno's great grandson and 1st Duke of Medina Sidonia, was left in control of Gibraltar. Four years later, however, King Enrique IV of Castile declared Gibraltar Crown property. Juan Alonso regained control temporarily but was finally ousted in 1501. Meanwhile, Algeciras across the bay was captured by the Christians from the Moors in 1344, lost to the Moors in 1370 and finally regained by Spain with the fall of Granada in 1492.

With the conflict between Moors and Christians finally resolved, peace reigned over the bay for over 200 years, until disturbed in 1704 by a violent 4-day battle that ensued on the arrival of the Anglo-Dutch fleet during the War of the Spanish Succession, and by the unsuccessful 4-month Spanish siege that followed.

Perhaps the most dramatic series of events spectators in the San Roque 'upper circle' would have witnessed occurred during the four years of the Great Siege which began in July 1779. The initial strategy seemed to be to isolate the Rock and starve the garrison into surrender. A fleet of gunboats based in Algeciras and Ceuta patrolled the Strait and cut off supplies from Morocco, and an army of nearly 14,000 threatened from beyond the isthmus. By the end of the year the garrison was suffering severe food shortages and morale was low, but just in time, in late January 1780, Admiral Rodney sailed into the bay with a convoy carrying food and other essential supplies, escorted by 21 ships of the line. For spectators in San Roque the arrival of the fleet must have been an impressive sight, but for the garrison it was much more than that: it was a life-saver, and cause for great rejoicing.

A different kind of spectacle was staged by the Spaniards in June 1779: the use of fire-ships. Nine ships (presumably past their 'sell-by' dates) were sent out from Algeciras on 7 June and directed at a few ships in the harbour that had broken through the gunboat blockade. As they neared the harbour they were set alight and abandoned. It must have been a spectacular show — which would have been even more spectacular had the ships not been intercepted and diverted from their targets.

Highlights of 1781 included the arrival of the second relief convoy, this time about 100 ships under the command of Admiral Darby; the heavy bombardment of the town from the batteries on the isthmus which was provoked by Darby's arrival and which continued throughout the following month, devastating most of the northern part of the town; and the famous Sortie of 27 November, when a force of 2600 men surprised the Spaniards on the isthmus in the early hours of the morning, destroyed their batteries and blew up their magazines.

But the greatest spectacle of the Great Siege was reserved for 13 September 1782. A French engineer by the name of Jean Claude Le Michaud d'Arçon had designed a floating battery that, he claimed, would withstand the heaviest cannonballs and also dampen out fires. Ten battery ships, carrying a total of 140 guns and 5200 men, were brought up within 800-900 yards of the Rock on the morning of 13 September, backed up by 49 ships of the Spanish and French fleets and by an army of 13,000 men on the isthmus. When the bombardment began from the battery ships and from the isthmus batteries (which had been rebuilt after the Sortie) the spectacle must have delighted the audience that had gathered around San Roque. The Spanish and French courts had been so confident of spectacular success that they publicized their battle plan across Europe, and among the crowd in San Roque were two French royal princes. Colonel John Drinkwater, an eye-witness and the first historian of the siege (*A History of the Late Siege of Gibraltar*, published in 1785) described the action as follows: "The showers of shot and shells which were now directed from their land batteries, the battery ships and, on the other hand, from the various works of the garrison, exhibited a scene of which perhaps neither the pen nor the pencil can furnish a competent idea". The weapon that was to prove decisive in the Rock's defence against the floating batteries was red-hot shot ('hot potatoes', as they were called) prepared in iron furnaces that had been specially constructed for the purpose. At first it seemed that d'Arçon's claims were justified, but by the afternoon the first signs of fire were seen and by midnight distress rockets were being fired. Tragic scenes followed, as the battery ships burst into flame, some exploding, and as their crews struggled for survival. It was like a huge firework display, but it was an absolute disaster, about 2000 Spaniards perishing in the inferno. The Rock had again proved that it was an impregnable fortress.

Hostilities finally ended on 2 February 1783. A month later, in admirable demonstrations of courtesy and mutual respect, the Duc de Crillon, commander of the Spanish and French forces, and Lieutenant-General George Augustus Eliott, Governor of Gibraltar, exchanged visits, Crillon touring the Rock and dining at The Convent (the Governor's residence) on 12 March and Eliott inspecting the isthmus batteries and dining in San Roque two weeks later.

Since 1783 Gibraltar has remained secure in British hands and nothing as spectacular as the events of 13 September 1782 has occurred in the bay. However, as an important naval base it has seen the comings and goings of great fleets, first during the war against Napoleon when the base played a vital part in enabling the great victory off Cape Trafalgar, then during the First and Second World Wars (especially the Second, when it was also a busy air base), and more recently during the Falklands and Gulf wars.

Images of some of these events in Gibraltar's history flooded through my mind as I gazed out from San Roque. There can be few places in the world that have generated so much military and naval conflict over so many years. Now the conflict is political. Spain wants the Rock and considers the wishes of the Gibraltarians irrelevant: Gibraltar insists on its right to self-determination which, after nearly 300 years as a British colony, is expressed strongly in favour of continued association with Britain. There seems to be little scope for compromise. Gibraltarians like myself love Spain but not her government's undemocratic policy towards us.

CHAPTER 19
A SHORT HOP TO THE ROCK
SAN ROQUE TO GIBRALTAR

It is only 8km from San Roque to Gibraltar but it was to be a special day marking a triumphant entry into Gibraltar. Leaving San Roque, a hill drops steeply to sea level, the Rock straight ahead, its north face rising impressively, almost vertically, to about 1300 feet. Free-wheeling down the hill I enjoyed that feeling of satisfaction, even pride, that comes from achieving a difficult objective. Months later I read an article by Matthew Parris in *The Times* in which he described his feelings on reaching the summit of a mountain in Bolivia. His words reflect exactly my own feelings on the approach to Gibraltar: "The thrill lay in the knowledge that I had done it. It had taken me close to the limits of my strength and endurance. I had feared that I might fail and I had not. It was as simple (and childish) as that: a personal victory". Leaving behind the smoking chimneys of the refinery, the road passes through the village of Campamento and then hugs the La Linea beach before reaching the Gibraltar frontier. Passing the few cars queueing to enter Gibraltar (cyclists are not required to join the queue), the *Viejo Equipo* at last crossed the finishing line. I passed quickly through the police and customs posts and waited on the other side — it was one of the few occasions on the trip that I had led the way. Looking back, I could see Roger being interviewed by Gibraltar customs officers; I thought they must have picked him out as a suspicious-looking character who might be carrying a few pounds of drugs in his panniers. This, however, was not the reason for the hold-up; my family had alerted the local television company, who had then asked the frontier officials to hold us there until their camera crew arrived. In due course we were interviewed and appeared in the local TV news programme later in the day — fame at last. A young German rode up on a bicycle and asked what we had done to attract such attention. When told he instantly offered himself for interview — he was cycling round the world, he said, not just through Spain. His offer was turned down: the modest achievement of a local 'boy' was of greater interest to Gib TV than the world exploits of a young German. Unfair perhaps — he certainly thought so.

After the interview we rode off, not risking the traditional race winner's both-hands-aloft-punching-the-air celebration in

The Rock from La Linea

case we fell off and were still being filmed. We crossed the air-field (which was built during the Second World War and runs east-west across the road), rode up on to the Line Wall Road, past The Convent (in Spanish times a Franciscan convent, in British the Governor's residence), through Southport Gate in the Charles V Wall (built in the reign of Charles V, Holy Roman Emperor, who was also Carlos I of Spain), and past the Trafalgar Cemetery (where many of the casualties of the great battle are buried). I had been a little surprised that my wife and sisters had not met us at the frontier, but now we were chased the rest of the way to my mother's home by their car wildly tooting its horn: a noisy welcome down the finishing straight. Like a marathon run-ner breaking the tape, finishing was a great relief but also some-thing of an anticlimax. The whole experience was suddenly a thing of the past, the excitement of the challenge instantly dissi-pated. The sense of satisfaction was tinged with some regret that it was all over. The deed was done and all that would be left were the memories. Roger's computer recorded that his daily average speed ranged from 11.2 mph to 16.5 mph, that his top speed was 38.2 mph (presumably charging downhill) and that we had cycled a total of 805 miles. Next morning there would be a long lie-in, and definitely no cycling.

The Rock is only $3^1/_2$ miles long, and only about three-quar-ters of a mile wide at its widest point (not including the large area recently reclaimed from the sea at the northern end of the harbour), but within that small area there is much of interest. Evidence of its history as a fortress is not hard to find. In an ele-vated position overlooking the isthmus are the remains of the Moorish castle, built in 1333. Along the western shore facing the harbour stand thick limestone walls which conceal a series of once-fortified bastions, the walls showing surprisingly little signs of the battering they must have received during the various sieges. Several old gun batteries remain; one of these (Princess Caroline's, built in 1732) stands above the Moorish Castle and now houses a small Military Heritage Centre containing among its exhibits a copy of a letter written by Lord Nelson to Emma Hamilton two days before the Battle of Trafalgar, and another (Parson's Lodge, a rocky promontory fortified since Moorish times) is south of the harbour, overlooking Rosia Bay where the *Victory* returned after the Battle of Trafalgar with Nelson's body preserved in a cask of brandy.

Perhaps most impressive of all the fortifications are the Great Siege Tunnels, which were created in 1782 under the direction of a Sergeant-Major Ince. Tunnelling was directed towards The Notch, a protuberance high on the sheer northern rock face east of Princess Caroline's battery, in order to establish positions from which guns could dominate the eastern part of the isthmus. As they progressed they blasted holes in the side of the tunnel for ventilation, and these openings provided the commanding positions they sought. It was a great engineering feat for which Ince is well remembered in Gibraltar.

Much of the old town was destroyed during the Great Siege, but it was rebuilt largely on the previous plan. Gradually it extended up the steep slope, and now the oldest part is a stack of tightly packed buidings (some sadly delapidated) linked by a maze of alleyways (many of which are stepped) rising up to the Moorish Castle and south to the Charles V Wall. The shop-lined Main Street, which runs north-south at the base of the slope from Casemates Square to Southport Gate, bustles with activity, especially from mid- to late mornings along its pedestrianized northern section, locals going about their business or simply out for a stroll mingling with tourists who have flooded in from Spain or been disgorged by a cruise liner. Young mothers push prams and pushchairs, parading their infants; senior citizens huddle in groups, enjoying a good joke or discussing the latest standoff with Spain; serious executive types in suits stride purposefully, briefcase in case and mobile phone on ear; and the tourists in often-ridiculous holiday outfits shuffle along, gazing into shop windows. The colourful scene is enlivened by a vibrant buzz generated by the multilingual voices of tourists and the Spanish and English of the locals (who mix Spanish and English words in almost every sentence — the uniquely Gibraltarian *llanito*), the buzz reverberating noisily within the confines of the narrow street, creating an ambience that cannot possibly be encountered elsewhere — it is quintessentially Main Street Gibraltar.

South beyond Southport Gate is the Alameda Botanical

Garden, and above it the road leads to the upper Rock, much of it now a Nature Reserve. Within the Reserve is the huge St Michael's Cave (large enough to be used for concerts and other events staged among spectacular stalactites and stalagmites), and the Barbary apes, symbols of British Gibraltar.

Until about 20 years ago much of the upper Rock was military property, out of bounds to civilians, but now almost all of it is accessible. A walk to the top of the Rock (about 1400ft) is one of the highlights of every visit I make to Gibraltar. The view is stupendous, rivalling any other in the world: to the north the hinterland beyond La Linea and San Roque; to the west, across the bay, Algeciras and the coast curving southwards and then west to the Atlantic; to the east the Mediterranean and the Costa del Sol; to the south the Strait of Gibraltar and beyond it the Moroccan coast from Ceuta to Tangier, the towering Djebel Musa especially prominent. It is awe-inspiring to stand there on top of one of the Pillars of Hercules, facing the other across the Strait which to the ancient Greeks and Romans marked the limit of the known world, to look north to one continent, south to another, east to one sea, west to another. It is a place in which to rejoice at being alive, to reflect on one's life, its past and its future. Roger and I were satisfied with our immediate past. The future? Contrary to some speculation that we would cycle back to Santander, we were packing up our bikes and flying home.

The top of the Rock, facing north

A Barbary ape

Djebel Musa across the Strait

149

EPILOGUE

I have experienced mixed feelings while writing this book: plea-sure in recalling events of a memorable journey, but also sadness because Roger, with whom I shared them, is no longer with us. He read an early draft of the book and encouraged me to perse-vere, but it was his untimely death that generated the strongest motivation to complete it, and to dedicate it to him.

He was the instigator of the challenge, driven by his bound-less energy and insatiable quest for action and excitement. No doubt other challenges would have followed. More than once he was heard to mumble about canoeing down the Yellow River. We laughed this off — but could he have been serious?